HOLD ON TO YOUR

N.U.T.s*

THE RELATIONSHIP MANUAL FOR MEN

WAYNE M. LEVINE, M.A.

BetterMen® Press

BetterMen® is a registered service mark, of WML, Inc., #3,028,424.
N.U.T.s™, Non-negotiable Unalterable Terms, is a trademark of WML. Inc.

Published in the United States by BetterMen® Press.

Submit all requests for reprinting to:
Greenleaf Book Group LP
4425 Mopac South, Suite 600, Longhorn Bldg., 3rd Floor, Austin, Texas 78735
(512) 891-6100

Design and composition by Greenleaf Book Group
Cover design by Greenleaf Book Group
Back cover photo by Everard Williams

Levine, Wayne M.
   Hold on to your N.U.T.s : the relationship manual for men / Wayne M. Levine. – 1st ed.

   p. ; cm.

   ISBN-13: 978-0-9790544-0-2
   ISBN-10: 0-9790544-0-0

   1. Men–Psychology. 2. Man-woman relationships. 3. Men–Family relationships. 4. Interpersonal relations. 5. Communication–Psychological aspects. I. Title.

HQ1090 .L48 2007
305.31   2006938210
ISBN 10: 0-9790544-0-0
ISBN 13: 978-0-9790544-0-2

First Edition
Printed in the United States of America

10 09 08 07   10 9 8 7 6 5 4 3 2 1

To Ria—
who has consistently supported and loved me
as I've worked to become a better man.
To Emma and Austin—
who make it all worthwhile.

CONTENTS

ACKNOWLEDGMENTS

My thanks go to:

Michael Nadeau, who first brought me to the men.

The hundreds of men who helped me become the man I am today—especially the men on my men's teams.

Larry Dutra, a consistent source of encouragement and insight who was with me from first draft to final manuscript.

Eddie Jacobs, my friend and mentor who helped me make sense of the lessons.

Mike Schwartzman, my most unlikely friend, mentor and guide. He led me, followed me, carried me, loved me and fathered me.

Paul Bob Velick, my friend and compadre whose creativity and passion have helped improve the lives of men, and the content of this book.

The men who have shared their experiences in this book.

Alex Miller, my editor, who found his N.U.T.s as he helped make this work accessible to other men.

Howard Fox, dedicated friend, team member and manuscript critic.

Dr. David J. Peck, ragtime pianist, biology teacher, author, friend and invaluable contributor to the manuscript.

Ariela Wilcox, for improving the structure of the manuscript and providing the coaching I needed to commit to the completion of the book.

David Davis, for his design and marketing expertise, friendship, and support in the work we do and in the development of the book.

Mike Kirby, for his friendship, generosity and creativity through the years.

Tony Rotundo, my old initiated friend and BetterMen.org web developer.

Dr. Vic Cohen, who helped me to be Wayne, in my life and in my work.

Dr. Barbara Dobrin, who supported my professional development and the creation of the West Coast Men's Center.

My many clients—men, women and kids—who taught me more than they will ever know.

My team at Greenleaf, who made this book look sweet, and helped to realize the vision.

Oma, for her unwavering generosity, love and support.

Emma, for being such a gift, and for teaching me that even when they're young, they're still women.

Austin, for giving me the best reason I have for becoming a better man, and for being a reminder—in so many fascinating ways—each and every time I fall short.

And Ria, my wife, partner, copy editor and friend for over 25 years, who always saw the better man, even when I was lost. Every man should be so lucky.

Thanks to all of you, this work is now available to more men who will hold on to their N.U.T.s and use the Tools as they become better men, husbands and fathers.

INTRODUCTION

Hold On to Your N.U.T.s *will help you gain a better understanding of yourself and of your relationships, supply the Tools needed to fix the problems, and teach you how to use these new and powerful Tools to make you happier and more successful in your relationships and in your life.*

ABOUT HOLD ON TO YOUR N.U.T.s

WHAT'S THE PURPOSE OF
HOLD ON TO YOUR N.U.T.s™?

Hold On to Your N.U.T.s is a relationship manual for men. It will help you to be happier and more successful in all of your relationships—husband, father, son, brother, friend, employer, employee . . . as a man. By working with the proven wisdom found in this book, you will develop a vision of the man you want to be. And by taking full responsibility for your relationships, and using the BetterMen® Tools, you will be on your way to becoming that better man.

Inside *Hold On to Your N.U.T.s* you're going to find two important sections. First, you will learn all about your N.U.T.s™—your **Non-negotiable, Unalterable Terms.** We're going to discuss what these are, how to develop them and how to maintain a firm grasp of them as you become the man you want to be.

Second, you'll learn the eight essential Tools every man needs to be happy in a successful relationship. The BetterMen Tools will help you to be the man you want to be—with his N.U.T.s intact—in your relationships and in your life.

> Chicken or the Egg?
> Taking full responsibility for your relationships means it's no longer important to know who did or said what first. It doesn't matter. All that matters is your commitment to being the best man you can be. So, start today, and don't be a chicken.

IS *HOLD ON TO YOUR N.U.T.s* ONLY FOR MEN?

Yes and no. The Tools are definitely for men. The information found inside these pages is just for you. The wisdom, advice, suggestions, and guidance are being handed down to you, man to man. And although women don't need to read this book, they, along with your children—current or future—and everyone else in your life, will be the beneficiaries of the better man you will become.

Hold On to Your N.U.T.s is also for men and women who are in the habit—or the profession—of helping men to be happier, healthier and more successful. This book is for therapists, counselors and friends. Anyone who cares about men will benefit from this time-tested work, as will the men they support. If you are currently in counseling, let your doctor or therapist know about the book. They can help you with the steps you'll be taking to be a better man in your relationships and in your life.

AM I THE ONLY MAN WHO NEEDS THIS BOOK?

You can be certain that you are not alone, not by a long shot. Men are not getting what they need on a number of levels. The divorce rate, the increased incidence of domestic violence, substance abuse, and the rage we see on the roads, in the work place and in our homes, all attest to this sad reality, as does the growing dependence on pharmaceuticals to manage the increased levels of depression and anxiety in our men.

Ask the women. They know what it's like living with unhappy men. Many men struggle with their relationships, careers and finances, finding themselves falling short of expectations. And then there are those men who seem to have it all—successful businesses, families, homes and toys—but are depressed, anxious, shut-down, angry and/or absent.

> We learn to be the best men we can be in the presence of other good men. Their wisdom, examples and support are indispensable for our journey through manhood.

Most men resist going to counseling. Those men who do seek help are sometimes seen by professionals who do not entirely understand what men need, or how to help them find it. Men don't always fit neatly into psychological theories or respond positively to one-size-fits-all techniques. Sadly, our men are getting more and more frustrated, angry, hostile, numb . . . and divorced. That's not good for our men, our women or our children.

Men need to be fathered and mentored to find solutions to their problems. I'll talk more later about what fathering means, why it is so crucial for men who want to be better men, husbands and fathers, and why fathering can only come from other men.

Even the most loving, generous and insightful women are often frustrated with the men they love. They may understand, love, and support their men, and they may even know what their men need. But they can't give it to them; they can't fix their men.

Many people will find themselves in couples counseling only to be disappointed with the results. Why? Because men have work to do on themselves first! If men are "dragged" to couples counseling before getting what they need—including being clear about their commitment to the relationship—little will be accomplished. Once they get what they need from other men, they are in a much better position to be active participants in their relationships—and in their relationship counseling. When the men are on board, couples can expect to see some positive, long-lasting results. Oftentimes, when men embrace their N.U.T.s and the BetterMen Tools, couples counseling is no longer necessary.

Granted, some relationships were never meant to be. But many troubled relationships can improve and even thrive when men commit to the process detailed in *Hold On to Your N.U.T.s.* Ultimately, the survival of any long-term relationship depends upon both partners' willingness to commit to the relationship and to supporting each other's efforts to self-improvement.

WHAT'S WAYNE'S STORY?

I'm from the Bronx. My dad worked at the post office and at a liquor store, while my mom took care of me and my two older brothers. We lived in a low-rent apartment in "the projects." Money was tight, and we moved around and followed the work.

We ended up in Connecticut. There were plenty of kids to play with in the leaves, the snow and the football fields.

I don't remember complaining. But I do remember being angry and getting into trouble—often. Although I was a smart kid, I had a problem following directions, respecting authority and "playing nice with others." I didn't realize it then, but my father issues were already calling the shots.

My dad didn't feel well. In fact, he was in pain quite a bit. I remember the smell of Heet, a liquid used to ease his back pain from an injury he'd sustained in the Navy. He worked. When he wasn't working, he read. When he wasn't reading, he hurt.

I found out later his back injury wasn't his only source of pain. All I knew then was that I had to fend for myself. Daddy wasn't available.

When I was seven, my dad bought tickets for my first Mets game. I was so excited. A couple days before, I had my appendix removed and we missed the game. He promised we'd go to another game. We never did. My father's pain consumed him, and the doctors couldn't find the source of it. Trips to the V.A. hospital and alternative practitioners filled my parents' days. After a while, it was suggested my dad see a psychiatrist. He was told his pain was psychosomatic.

As it turned out, my father's pain was real. At age 43, my dad died of pancreatic cancer. His name was Albert Levine.

I didn't visit the hospital that day, but I had a feeling. My mom came home and told me "Your father's not coming home." I remember my middle brother crying. I don't remember my mother crying, only her anger toward my father for dying and leaving her with three boys and no money. I didn't cry at the funeral, following my mom's lead of disconnecting, stuffing the feelings and running away.

We soon packed up, left the East Coast, and moved to Arizona. My mom wanted to leave it all behind. And she did. She rarely ever spoke of my dad again and then wondered later why I couldn't remember him. I didn't grieve my father's death until I was 33. That was when the men came into my life and I was **initiated into manhood**.

At various times since adolescence I struggled with anxiety and bouts of depression. In high school, they sent me to the nurse's office and then to my guidance counselor. He was a great guy, but he had no idea what was brewing inside of me.

My demons followed me to college. Although I always performed well in school, my depression was just an anxiety away. I never sought help. I just dealt with it, alone. Others rarely caught on.

> Most of the obstacles you face now to being a good man, husband and father can be traced back to your boyhood experiences. Becoming a better man will require you to silence that little boy.

In time, I started a business and a family. The responsibilities increased, along with the fears. Around the time of my daughter's first birthday, I became overwhelmed and severely depressed. My psychologist wanted to talk about my mother. My psychiatrist, well, all he had to offer were drugs. I eventually rejected the "help" and the drugs. As in the past, the depression lifted and I moved on.

Years later, a friend suggested I come to an open house of his "men's team." I had no idea what it was about, but I trusted him and knew he had a great passion for this "men's work" he often spoke of.

What I experienced that night changed my life. I heard men talking with each other in ways I had never heard before—honest, revealing, and shockingly supportive. All I knew was that I wanted some of that. My initiation into manhood had begun.

It wasn't until I developed trusting relationships with men that I truly began to heal, to understand what my pain was about, and to learn how to move beyond it. It wasn't until I accepted the wisdom of other men that I began to be a better father and husband. It wasn't until I made the commitment to break through my personal barriers that I learned to trust my gut and be the man I always wanted to be. It wasn't until my initiation into manhood that I came to see myself as man, not as a boy.

More than a decade after my journey with the men began, I've changed careers, earned a master's degree in clinical psychology, and have found my higher purpose in the work I do mentoring men.

WHERE DID THE BETTERMEN TOOLS COME FROM?

It was while earning my master's that I discovered a significant void in the curriculum: There wasn't a single class offered focusing on the specific needs of men. My purpose became clearer. Over the next several years, I reviewed my experiences—and those of the men I had encountered—compiled the many bits of wisdom I had received through my studies and from my mentors, and then began writing it all down.

As director of the West Coast Men's Center, where our mission is to make good men better, I mentor, teach, coach and father men, boys and men's groups. Through Mentor-4Men.com, I mentor men from around the world—by phone—and help them to become the men they want to be.

I also lead a team of men who facilitate the BetterMen® Retreats. These retreats offer men the opportunity to become the men they want to be—and to be initiated into manhood—through an intense and wildly exhilarating experience with other committed men. My concept of N.U.T.s—Non-negotiable, Unalterable Terms, and the BetterMen Tools, emerged from this work with the men that began over a decade ago.

> It takes courage to do this work because it's not yet "socially acceptable" for men to reach out to each other and to ask for help. But it's time we do just that—for ourselves, our families and society.

I've come to learn what actually works for men, and therefore for women and relationships. I've seen men and women at the "ends of their ropes" make dramatic turnarounds both individually and in their relationships. And the catalyst has primarily been the men having the courage to bring the BetterMen Tools to their relationships. These Tools can work quickly and—with commitment and perseverance—lead to permanent improvements in your relationships.

Everything you will find in this book is supportive of men, women and relationships. Although women will derive value from this manual, the words, ideas, support and suggestions are for the men. Until the men receive the help they need, marriages will continue to fail unnecessarily, families will crumble, children will be hurt and scarred, the pain will follow everyone involved into their future relationships, and too many of us will be prevented from living lives of true purpose, love and happiness.

WHY TOOLS?

We men love our tools, screwdrivers, wrenches, hammers, pliers, power tools and the like. But what tools do you use when

- There's something going on with you that's got you stumped, in fear, in pain, angry, or at the end of your rope?
- You find yourself in a perpetual state of arguing with your wife . . . or others?
- You realize your sex life has all but disappeared?
- Your moodiness and your "need to be right" get the best of you at home, or at the office?
- You need the support to act like a man—instead of a little boy—to be a positive example to your children?
- You feel you just haven't been taught the lessons you need to have healthy relationships as a husband, father, or friend?

Men need Tools for their relationships. We need support when we're not sure what we're doing. And when there's a problem we need to understand what's not working, and have access to the Tools needed to fix it. *Hold On to Your N.U.T.s* will help you gain a better understanding of yourself and of your relationships, supply the Tools needed to fix the problems, and teach you how to use these new

> It's not enough to read this book. You've got to get into action. Take advantage of the BetterMen® Actions you'll find accompanying each of the BetterMen Tools. Men are judged by their actions. Everything else is just words.

and powerful Tools to make you happier and more successful in your relationships and in your life.

A NOTE ABOUT STYLE

You'll notice that when describing N.U.T.s and the BetterMen Tools, I'll usually refer to husbands and wives. I happen to be heterosexual and in a traditional married relationship. But the material in *Hold On to Your N.U.T.s* is equally relevant for men who are dating—or considering dating—and seeking a long-term relationship, and for gay, bi or any other men who want to have happier and more loving relationships. The BetterMen Tools—this age-old wisdom—transcends labels and sexual orientation. This is for all men ready to be the men they want to be in all their relationships.

HOW TO USE *HOLD ON TO YOUR N.U.T.s*

There are two ways for you to use *Hold On to Your N.U.T.s*:

Cover-to-Cover It's a short book, so you can read it all pretty quickly. In fact, you may want to read it a few times. You're bound to discover important information, fatherly advice and other tips that will help you make sense of your current relationships and guide you toward fixing them.

Be random Just open the book. When a topic catches your eye, stop. There's probably something there for you to learn about you as a man and about you as a man in your relationships.

In addition to learning about N.U.T.s and the Better-Men Tools, you'll also discover BetterMen Actions to support each of the eight Tools. These BetterMen Actions are designed to help you take the ideas found here and integrate them into your life as soon as possible. And for added support, you'll find Tools In Use, first-hand accounts of how men—just like you—are using the BetterMen Tools to improve their relationships. Along the way, you'll also find some helpful Warnings! and Tips! like the one on the following page.

If you stay committed to and apply the lessons learned from *Hold On to Your N.U.T.s*, you will make significant changes in you, and in your life. Once you begin to master the lessons here, you will find something better on the other side: the man you want to be, in relationships that work. Good luck, and don't quit!

TIP!

Hold On To Your N.U.T.s is designed to be read quickly—on the john, between appointments or during commercials. Stick it in your glove compartment, in your briefcase, or near your recliner for easy access.

It may take a while to integrate this wisdom into your life. The more you refer to this book, and the more you practice, the sooner you'll be the man you want to be in your relationships and in your life.

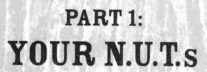

PART 1:
YOUR N.U.T.s

Your N.U.T.s define you as a man. When you compromise your N.U.T.s, your Non-negotiable, Unalterable Terms, you compromise yourself!

YOUR N.U.T.s

WHAT ARE N.U.T.s?

N.U.T.s are your Non-negotiable, Unalterable Terms. N.U.T.s are the things you're committed to, the things that matter more than anything else: your kids, your work, yourself, your purpose, your spiritual practice, your hobbies, your integrity, your morals and your psychological well-being.

N.U.T.s are the boundaries that define you as man, those things which, if repeatedly compromised, will gradually—but assuredly—turn you into a pissed-off, resentful man who will likely blame others—especially your wife—for your unhappiness.

Your N.U.T.s are uniquely yours. They reflect who you are as a man and the man you want to be. Compromise your N.U.T.s, and you'll compromise yourself. Compromise yourself too often, and you'll become an extremely unhappy man, husband and father.

SAMPLE N.U.T.s

Here's a short list of Non-negotiable, Unalterable Terms provided by the men of our BetterMen community. These will give you an idea of the N.U.T.s which men, like you, have developed for themselves in their efforts to be the men they want to be.

I am faithful to my wife.

I say what I want.

Compassion for my family
trumps my need to be right.

I replace doubt with acts of faith.

I am a risk taker.

I devote at least three hours
a week to my writing.

I will only seek validation from the men.

I live in accordance with my religious faith.

I do what I believe is in the best interest
of my kids, even if they disagree.

My commitment to my children
comes before everything else.

Patience over temper.

I do not ask for permission.

Fear does not keep me from taking risks.

I do not indulge my addictions.

I am a man of my word—period!

I take my problems to men, not to women.

I do not show anger to my elderly mother.

I do not tolerate my wife's
attempts to belittle me.

When name-calling begins,
the discussion is over.

I spend time with the men.

I have my own private office/space
some place in my house.

I exercise regularly.

I do whatever it takes to keep
my family in our home.

I ask for help when I'm not being
the man I want to be.

I speak my mind in spite of my
fear of confrontation.

I honor my daily spiritual practice.

I welcome feedback.

I only apologize when it's appropriate,
not simply to please others.

I do not hide out at work just
to avoid issues at home.

I decide how I interact with my boys.

I choose which of my friendships to maintain.

I do not sell out who I am to placate others.

I share my men's work with the men in my life.

I do as I see fit.

This list is here simply to inspire you. Maybe some of these N.U.T.s resonate with you. If so, use them and make them your own. But perhaps your N.U.T.s aren't listed above. Do you know what they are? Not sure? No problem. Let's talk first about how a man finds his N.U.T.s.

FINDING YOUR N.U.T.s

NEVER COMPROMISE YOUR N.U.T.s

Understanding the importance of finding and never compromising your N.U.T.s—your Non-negotiable, Unalterable Terms—is the most important thing you, as a man, will do. This may be the most important lesson you will learn from *Hold On to Your N.U.T.s*. So here it is:

> Once you find your N.U.T.s, never forget them and never compromise them.

For some men, that may sound like great advice, a few years too late. But it's not too late. What you read here will help. In fact, men just like you have turned their lives and their relationships around because they've committed themselves to finding their N.U.T.s and maintaining a firm grasp of their Non-negotiable, Unalterable Terms.

OK, so now that you understand what N.U.T.s are, how do you get started finding yours? Some men find their N.U.T.s over time, while others sit down and make a list. Either way, here are some of the questions you'll want to ask yourself:

- What's most important to me in life?
- Are there activities I used to do for fun that I no longer do? Is someone interfering and am I resentful because of it?
- Are there valuable friendships with men I've let slip away?
- Where am I currently having problems (unhappy, frustrated, sad, angry, resentful) in my life, and did compromising myself—and what's important to me—contribute to my feelings and/or the situation?
- What dreams have I abandoned?
- If I'm going to be the man I want to be, what will I have to do differently?

> ## TIP!
>
> Having trouble understanding what a N.U.T. feels like? Try this: You're walking down the street with your young daughter and a stranger grabs her, intending to kidnap her. How do you feel about that? Is giving up your daughter acceptable? Could you be persuaded to see the advantages of giving your daughter to a stranger? No? Of course not! In fact, you don't even have to consider it. It's very clear to you: You don't let strangers take your daughter! It's non-negotiable and unalterable. It's a term of yours. You have a N.U.T. How about that!
>
> That's how clear your N.U.T.s must eventually be for you. Your N.U.T.s must be so ingrained that you don't even consider them when challenged. They just are.

Some men may have a hard time identifying their N.U.T.s on their own and would benefit from the support of other men. (That's why Develop Trusting Relationships with Men is one of the BetterMen Tools.) In men's groups, many men will find their N.U.T.s by hearing from others who have had similar challenges, men who have identified their own Non-negotiable, Unalterable Terms.

PROTECT YOUR N.U.T.s

Once you've identified your N.U.T.s, you'll most likely have a short list of Non-negotiable, Unalterable Terms. Remembering them should not be a problem. Remembering to live them, however, is where you will be challenged.

Keep your N.U.T.s close to the vest—and review them daily—until you're ready to live them. (By all means, share them with the men in your life who can help to define your N.U.T.s and then support you when you're ready to put them into action.)

Sharing your N.U.T.s prematurely is often an indication of your need for approval. You may be tempted to mention your N.U.T.s to your woman to test her reaction, and to see what resistance you may be up against. Also, receiving permission to live your N.U.T.s defeats their purpose.

Again, N.U.T.s are to be lived, not discussed. So resist the temptation to talk about your N.U.T.s with those who ultimately will be impacted by them. Wait until you're ready, and then live them.

> Remember, you can't ask for permission to be the man you want to be, you simply have to be that man.

MAINTAINING A FIRM GRASP OF YOUR N.U.T.s

To better understand what N.U.T.s are and how they work, take a look at the things in your life you're not happy with. You may be unhappy with your relationship with your wife, your kids or your parents. You may be unhappy with relationships at work or with work in general. You may just be unhappy about being unhappy, or afraid, sad, angry or lonely.

Let's say, for example, you're contemplating divorce because you just can't live with your wife anymore. You've had it! And last night was the final straw—she "made you" miss your weekly basketball night with the men because she was upset at you for forgetting to run an important errand. You apologize. But tonight, that's not enough for her. She believes a truly caring, apologetic husband would cancel his night out with his buddies. So, instead of being the man you want to be—apologizing and then sticking with your plans—you stay home, cop an attitude and make everyone around you miserable.

This is an example of allowing yourself to be compromised because you weren't clear about your N.U.T.s. Your term around your basketball game was negotiable, apparently. It wasn't a N.U.T. and you **sold it out**, minimized its importance, dishonored your commitment to yourself and your buddies, and rationalized to keep the peace. Why?

Maybe because you felt guilty, didn't want to deal with her being upset, wanted to avoid another confrontation, or because you felt it was the "right thing" to do. But you did it, and now you resent her for "making" you do it.

If your N.U.T. had been

I play basketball with my buddies once a week,

---

you would not have compromised or negotiated it away so easily, just because she was unhappy with you. Instead of becoming increasingly more resentful, you could have been more available to deal directly with what caused the tension between the two of you, which had nothing to do with your basketball night. Remember? It was about not having done her errand.

Underneath it all, it might have been about her not being able to count on you and how that makes her feel. It would have been very helpful for the two of you to have had that conversation. Instead, you compromised your N.U.T.s and nothing productive took place.

See how this cycle works? When you hold on to your N.U.T.s, the cycle stops. The potential for resentment to build is minimized. You have an opportunity to work things out with your wife in the moment. No need to call in the lawyers.

MEN FEAR THEIR WOMEN

One of the main reasons a man is reluctant to establish his N.U.T.s is because of the fear he has of his woman, and of his woman's reactions. When he imagines himself making changes in his relationship, he's often terrified of how he **thinks** his wife will respond. If a man believes his N.U.T.s will upset her in any way, cause tension between them, or lead to another night on the couch, his fears will be major obstacles to bringing his N.U.T.s to his relationship.

But beyond fearing their wives, men are also afraid of their own reactions in response to their women. They don't trust themselves. They're afraid their actions will lead to an argument and a big mess—so why bother?

Maybe it's becoming clearer to you why you should bother. If you don't find your N.U.T.s, and hold on to them in your relationships, it will slowly eat at you and strain your relationships.

But there's more. In addition to feeling better about yourself and honoring what's most important to you, you will also become a man your wife will have a reason to respect. You'll become a man who knows who he is, honors his commitments and never compromises his N.U.T.s.

She may not always be happy with your choices. She may even be angry with you from time to time. But she'll know that she can count on you. And most women will admit—at least to their girlfriends—that's an attractive quality in a man.

FEELING COMPROMISED?

How compromised have you felt over the years because your actions were based on someone else's terms, expectations or desires? Has it happened at home, at the office, with your kids, your parents or in volunteer work? What would it mean to you to do things, to follow through, to act or to speak according to what seems best to you, as you see fit?

Sure, it would be freeing! If your Non-negotiable, Unalterable Terms were clear to you, you wouldn't make a move until you were certain it was in alignment with who you are, and reflected the man you want to be.

HONOR YOUR FEELINGS

There are so many ways in which men deny their feelings. You're probably aware of some of them. Why do you do it? Perhaps you've gotten used to not being heard, not getting what you want, getting hurt if you express yourself, or getting into "trouble" for expressing yourself the "wrong" way. As a result, you've adapted. You've learned to identify which behaviors attract the heat and which don't.

In an effort to avoid the drama, confrontation or other uncomfortable feelings, you've learned to avoid those situations. Now, it's difficult for you to access your feelings, or you simply rationalize them away. In doing so, you've gradually lost track of your true feelings, passions, desires,

WARNING!

Having N.U.T.s doesn't mean you always get to do what you want, when you want. Once you have your N.U.T.s, in fact, you'll find yourself easily cooperating in ways you never imagined.

In addition, if you want to have a healthy, loving, long-term relationship, there are several things you'll need to do specifically for her. Read on.

hopes and dreams. You've **settled**. You've compromised yourself, or as we say in our BetterMen work, you've **sold yourself out**. In short, you've lost track of your N.U.T.s.

The good news is that you can find those N.U.T.s again. And once you do, you'll use them as a roadmap to live the life you want as the man you want to be.

A MAN WITH N.U.T.s COOPERATES

Once you know your N.U.T.s and to never compromise them, you'll be free to cooperate in those areas where your N.U.T.s are secure. For instance, you're not compromising your N.U.T.s when you go to the restaurant or movie she wants to go to. You're not compromising your N.U.T.s when you delay washing your boat because she's in the dumps and needs her man to hear her unload. In fact, being a good listener is an important BetterMen Tool.

TIP!

Wondering what it looks like when a man holds on to his N.U.T.s? Have you seen Charlton Heston in *The Ten Commandments*? Heston, as Moses, descends from Mt. Sinai with two stone tablets he says were inscribed by God. He was serious. And although some challenged him, did you see him budge? Not for a second! Sure, there was a great soundtrack and fabulous new highlights in his hair, but it was his attitude, his unshakeable belief, that convinced everyone.

Your N.U.T.s need to be as set in stone as were those commandments. You need to honor and hold on to your N.U.T.s just as Heston, I mean Moses, honored and held those commandments. They were non-negotiable and unalterable. Honoring your N.U.T.s will have an equally dramatic impact on your life.

N.U.T.s VS. CONDITIONS

It is critical for you to understand the difference between a N.U.T. and a condition. Here's a healthy N.U.T. for you to bring to your relationship:

I exercise every day.

It's important to you, it's part of who you are and it's not up for discussion. You will find a way to make this work, and it may require juggling other responsibilities or schedules. But regardless of the circumstances in your life, you're clear that this is a Non-negotiable, Unalterable Term.

Here's a condition:

I don't do the dishes.

This is the little boy digging in his heels because the man compromised himself so long ago—or he never learned the difference between a N.U.T. and a condition. All he's got left, he thinks, is to hold on to whatever he can. So he makes a big deal out of making the bed, or putting out the trash, or some other trivial item—any way to "get back" at her or to let her know he can't be "bossed around." Psychologists call this passive-aggressive behavior. Unfortunately, a lot of men are very good at this—and that's very bad for relationships.

BEING A MAN IS NOT CONDITIONAL

A man who enforces conditions is a man who is not clear and confident about who he is as a man. He's concerned about his woman getting the best of him, having to do something for her that he hates, or is simply full of resentment. In other words, he blames her for his sorry state and is going to "draw the line" to prove he's in charge. As

WARNING!

Learn to tell the difference between a man's N.U.T.s—his terms—and a little boy's conditions. Your N.U.T.s define you as a man in a positive way. Conditions define what the resentful, hurt and angry little boy inside of you will or won't do from a negative and defensive position, so there! If you can imagine yourself stomping your feet and whining while you tell her, it's not a N.U.T. And remember, N.U.T.s are never defended; they're just lived.

You'll constantly be tested to compromise your N.U.T.s when your terms conflict with the desires of others. Defending them and engaging in a protracted discussion explaining your N.U.T.s will only weaken your position. As Popeye would say, "I y'am what I y'am!"

a five-year-old boy would say, "You're not the boss of me!" And a man acting like a five-year-old is not cute. Worse, it's destructive and will push away the ones he loves.

Here are a few examples of N.U.T.s versus conditions. This will help you to know the difference between the two as you take an inventory of the man you want to be.

You're free to take from, add to or completely disregard our sample N.U.T.s. Your N.U.T.s are yours and they should come from within. These are commitments that you intend to honor, no matter the circumstances, no matter the tests, no matter the pain. Your N.U.T.s define you as a man. When you compromise your N.U.T.s, your Non-negotiable, Unalterable Terms, you compromise yourself!

N.U.T.s (for the powerful man)	vs.	CONDITIONS (for the resentful little boy)
My family attends religious services weekly.		We only go to the 10 a.m. service.
I support my wife in her choice of friends.		I do not go to parties where I have to put up with her friends' boring husbands.
I exercise regularly.		I go to the gym when it's convenient for me.
I am "present" with my family when I return home from work.		If she doesn't piss me off during the day, I'll help her out when I get home.
I'm committed to not sweating the small stuff.		There's peace in the house as long as I find my tools right where I left them.
People will treat each other with respect in our home.		As man of the house, I'll do what I damn well please.

TESTING YOUR N.U.T.s

Make no mistake; you will be tested. It may be your wife, your kids, your work or any number of other people or circumstances. That's why you have these N.U.T.s; so when you are tested by life, and the desires, needs or self-serving motives of others, you'll remain intact—the man you want to be. That's why it is crucial for you to hold on to your N.U.T.s and to be completely OK with them and their potential consequences.

When you embrace them without reservation and without conditions, you won't get angry when they're tested. You'll be able to respond—if a response is necessary—calmly and even lovingly as you let the "tester" know that "it ain't gonna happen."

As a man in one of our men's groups put it, "Having N.U.T.s is the opposite of being wishy-washy, my great failing."

COMMITMENTS ELIMINATE DOUBT

The beautiful thing about identifying our N.U.T.s and making the commitment to never compromise them is that our lives become much simpler. When we commit to something, we no longer have to struggle with a choice. The choice has already been made. We made it. Life becomes a little more black and white, which is what commitments are all about, what our N.U.T.s are all about. The commitment frees us from doubt and allows us to redirect our energies to more positive endeavors, like being present with our children and our wives, focusing on our work, enjoying our time alone, and feeling good about the men we are becoming.

CHALLENGES TO YOUR N.U.T.s

Once you've identified your N.U.T.s and have committed to integrating them into your life, it'll be frustrating when you run into the inevitable obstacles.

Few people like change. Many dread it. The first person you'll have to be concerned with is **you**. All of your fears are going to come up. All of your anxieties will race into action to defend against those feelings of fear, to cloud the issue, to throw you into doubt, confusion and laziness. The voices, the old scripts, that little devil on your shoulder, all will try to give you every reason to quit.

Making these changes to be the man you want to be is going to be work. And this work will require you to get out of your comfort zone, for sure. It's going to require you

> Your own unresolved issues will be your first challenge, the first test of your newly acquired N.U.T.s.

to be clear, committed and consistent. You may not always do a good job, you may slip, and you may look like a jerk in your initial attempts to live your N.U.T.s. **All of these missteps are normal.**

You'll be making changes that will elicit reactions from those around you. You may be worried about those reactions, and you may doubt your ability to hold your ground in the face of those reactions. This is all to be expected. Applying your N.U.T.s will take practice, practice and more practice. It'll take time for those around you—and maybe even you—to trust that these new behaviors are permanent; that they're actually non-negotiable and unalterable.

Eventually, you'll experience a victory. You'll get filled up with the success of holding on to your N.U.T.s and not compromising them. This win will lead to another. And soon, you'll realize you're becoming the man you want to be and are happier as a result. Most likely, those around you will come to be happier, too. Sounds good, doesn't it?

WHAT A WIN LOOKS LIKE

So what would a victory look like in this battle to establish your N.U.T.s? Let's say your N.U.T. is

---

I am a supportive and
loving husband.

That commitment requires you to use the BetterMen Tools, one of which is Listen. You sit with your wife in the kitchen and she tells you about her day and maybe a few things that are bothering her. As she goes through her list, she mentions a thing or two about YOU! Suddenly, your pulse rate goes up or you feel that tightness in your chest or that constriction in your throat. You find yourself taking your wife's comments personally. You forget your N.U.T.s. You forget everything you've read in this book. You get defensive or combative and the old familiar patterns repeat themselves. You find yourself arguing. You lose.

But you don't quit. As the BetterMen Tools suggest, you take it to the men to get the support you need.

A few days later you sit down with her again. She tells you about her day. Her list reappears. But this time you're better prepared. You remember your BetterMen Tools. You remind yourself what it means to be a good listener. She tells you what's on her mind. You listen. Then she hugs you, or simply continues preparing dinner. Now you're sort of confused. You're wondering, what just happened? And then it hits you: You didn't have an argument. You successfully implemented the BetterMen Tools to not argue and to be a good listener, and honored your N.U.T. to be a supportive and loving husband. You didn't make it about you, take what she had to say personally, try to fix her problems, get defensive or storm off in anger.

You just let her talk. You held on to your N.U.T.s. You're proud of yourself. You now realize that what once seemed impossible was actually quite manageable—and you did it! It feels good. And that feeling—that win—is what fills you up and motivates you to continue on your journey to be the man you want to be—a man who holds on to his N.U.T.s.

> Your second challenge, if you're already in a long-term relationship, may be standing by your N.U.T.s while under her microscope.

If she wants you to make changes that are in your best interest, and quite possibly hers as well, you're a fortunate man. (Just make sure they're **your** N.U.T.s and **not** hers. That's another common way men sell themselves out.) But it still won't be a cakewalk. If she's not supportive, and her anger, resentment and unresolved issues make her resistant to your changes, you may be in for a bumpy ride.

THIS WORK IS FOR YOU

This is a good time to point out that being the man you want to be has to be, first and foremost, for you. If you're trying to make these changes to make her happy, forget it. You'll never make it. Being a pleaser has rarely worked for you in the past, right? All you've accomplished is temporarily satisfying others at the expense of what you want—selling yourself out.

What we're talking about here is making fundamental changes in you as a man. You have to commit to making these changes because **you** want to make them—even though they'll ultimately benefit those you care about. If you're doing this for others, you'll base your success or failure in this process on their reactions. Especially in the early stages, others' reactions to your new N.U.T.s are not the barometer you need to assess your progress—although there is often much to learn through the reactions your N.U.T.s elicit. What matters is how **you** feel you're doing.

Often times, others will not initially act favorably to you and your N.U.T.s. That's why this work has to be for you, first. If your commitment is strong, you'll be able to slowly integrate your N.U.T.s, no matter the resistance. But, you may ask, what if she's never supportive of me and persists in trying to crush my N.U.T.s? Yeah, that's a good question.

NO GUARANTEES

There's no guarantee that when you become the man you want to be, she'll like or want to be with that man. You can't control the outcome of this important process. If you're doing this to be a better man, husband, father or friend, good will come of it. The challenge for you will be to stay committed to this uncertain process of change in the face of your fears, doubts and apprehensions. The end game is your happiness, and being the husband, father and man you've always wanted to be.

Many men come to counseling already sure divorce is the only reasonable option for them. They're miserable, have been so for a long time, and are convinced "she's to blame." Or maybe they think she's not entirely to blame but that there's really no point in "prolonging the inevitable."

In the BetterMen process, men are encouraged to use their troubled marriages as a laboratory. After all, since they're on the brink of throwing in the towel, what have they got to lose? The truth is, whatever your contribution to the situation, it will undoubtedly be repeated in your future relationships—unless you learn the lessons. Your challenge, then, is to recommit to the relationship long enough to apply the BetterMen Tools consistently, and to see if your efforts can have a positive effect on your relationship, and on your own happiness.

WOMEN RESPOND TO MEN WHO USE THE TOOLS

Some men are astonished at how quickly their wives respond to their healthier behaviors, whether it's being a better listener, not arguing or running the sex and romance departments—three of the BetterMen Tools. They are equally amazed at their own changes in attitude toward their wives. Suddenly, she's not as unattractive as he had grown to believe, she's not actually gunning for him relentlessly as he had perceived, or she's actually wanting him to be closer to her, not to feel pushed away.

But then there's the flip side. Some men learn that no matter how hard they try, their wives cannot or will not participate in improving the relationship, whether it's forgiving their men, seeking out individual counseling or following through on suggestions received in marriage therapy. Sometimes, the right choice is to end the relationship.

But if leaving is the decision, it is critical for men to know that they had done their absolute best; that they had succeeded in making personal changes and can honestly say that they had been the men they wanted to be in their relationships. This can be a very difficult task.

WARNING!

Your children are watching your every move. Their beliefs and futures are being molded by the choices you make. Your sons will grow up to be men like you. Your daughters will marry men like you. That's why, as a father, being the man you want to be is the most important legacy you will leave to your children.

In most cases, men need a great deal of guidance, support and encouragement to do their best in the face of the state of their relationships, their own negative feelings, and their overwhelming urge to end the pain and to just get out. That's why Develop Trusting Relationships with Men is one of the BetterMen Tools.

If there are no children involved, it's obviously much easier to call it quits, although the same issues will resurface in future relationships. But if there are kids, **it is a man's duty to protect them and to know that, without doubt, he is doing what is in their best interest.**

Sometimes that will mean ending a marriage and beginning a new life as a healthier man and father, and teaching your children valuable lessons about life, marriage and parenting. But if you're like most men who seek help, it's probably too soon to make that important decision. That's why this book is for you. The Tools and wisdom you'll find here will help you to know, with certainty, whether to leave or to do your best to turn your relationship around and to create a safe, loving and nurturing home for your kids and their parents.

It will be important for you to come to terms with the questions and uncertainty this brings up as you go about integrating your N.U.T.s. The support you receive throughout this process will be crucial. That support can come from friends, family, a mentor or your men's group. Using the eight essential BetterMen Tools—detailed a few pages from now—and reaching out for help will see you through this process.

If it were easy, everyone would be doing it. Look around. Few men have the courage to do this work. You're one of them. Don't quit.

APPLYING YOUR N.U.T.s

Once you're clear about your N.U.T.s, your reasons for wanting to integrate them into your life, and the potential resistance you'll face, it's time to put your N.U.T.s into action.

Here's the most important thing to remember about being the man you want to be and holding on to your N.U.T.s:

> Don't talk about
> your N.U.T.s, just live them.

A man is judged by his actions—period. The more words you use, the more opportunity there will be for others to challenge them. I'll say it again: Don't talk about your N.U.T.s, just live them.

You now know what your N.U.T.s are, and you're ready to apply them in your relationships and in your life. How do you do that? How successful you are at holding on to your N.U.T.s will largely depend on how well you follow through on using the BetterMen Tools. Committing yourself to your N.U.T.s and putting the BetterMen Tools to use will help you show up as the man you want to be: the husband, the father, the employer, the employee, the friend.

IN A N.U.T.SHELL

LET'S RECAP YOUR N.U.T.s:

- N.U.T.s are your Non-negotiable, Unalterable Terms, those things that you're committed to and that define you as man.

- Commitments make life easier by eliminating doubt and making our choices black and white.

- Repeatedly compromising your N.U.T.s will piss you off.

- Take the sample N.U.T.s and make some of them your own, or develop new N.U.T.s that better reflect the man you want to be.

- To develop your own N.U.T.s, start by asking yourself tough questions to discover where you've sold yourself out in the past.

- Ultimately, you'll want your N.U.T.s to be so ingrained that you don't even pause to consider them when challenged.

- A men's group is a great place to develop your N.U.T.s.

- Once you find your N.U.T.s, never forget them and never compromise them.

- You don't ask for permission to be the man you want to be.

- Resist the temptation to discuss your N.U.T.s—other than with the men. Just live them.

- Maintaining a firm grasp of your N.U.T.s will help you break through whatever fear you may have of your woman and her reactions.

- A man knows the difference between N.U.T.s and little boy-like conditions.

- If you don't find your N.U.T.s, and hold on to them in your relationships, it will slowly eat at you and strain your relationships.

- As a man who holds on to his N.U.T.s, she may not always be happy with you. But she will learn to respect you and, over time, respect your N.U.T.s.

- Having N.U.T.s doesn't mean you'll always get what you want when you want it.

- Your N.U.T.s are like your Ten Commandments.

- Once you know your N.U.T.s and don't compromise them, you'll be free to cooperate in those areas where your N.U.T.s are secure.

- A man with N.U.T.s is judged by how he responds to the inevitable tests he'll face when challenged by people and circumstances.

- Your own unresolved issues will be your first challenge, and the first test of your newly acquired N.U.T.s.

- Being under her microscope will also be a major test. Focus on doing this work for you, and give her time to learn to trust this new man you're becoming.

- You may be astonished by how quickly your loving woman will respond to her man, the one who's now holding on to his N.U.T.s.

- Applying your N.U.T.s will take practice, practice and more practice. You're bound to slip up from time to time. Have patience with yourself.

- Being the man you want to be is the most important legacy you will leave to your children.

- There are no guarantees about where this work will take you. Do the work and have faith that good will come of your efforts. Don't quit.

Let's take a look at the BetterMen Tools and talk about how putting these eight essential Tools to use consistently will help you to be the man you want to be in your relationships and in your life.

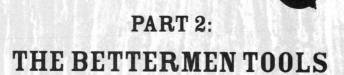

PART 2:
THE BETTERMEN TOOLS

*To be the man you want
to be in your relationships,
you'll need some powerful Tools.*

THE BETTERMEN TOOLS

Consistent use of the BetterMen Tools will help you to hold on to your N.U.T.s and be the man you want to be in your successful, long-term relationships.

1. **SILENCE THE LITTLE BOY**
2. **EXPRESS BUT DON'T DEFEND YOUR FEELINGS**
3. **COOPERATE WITHOUT COMPROMISING YOUR N.U.T.s**
4. **RUN THE SEX AND ROMANCE DEPARTMENTS**
5. **BE THE ROCK**
6. **DON'T ARGUE**
7. **LISTEN**
8. **DEVELOP TRUSTING RELATIONSHIPS WITH MEN**

Most of you have heard phrases like "She's got his balls," and "He's married to a real ballbuster." Well, after grasping your own N.U.T.s and learning to use the BetterMen Tools, you'll be in a much better position to see that these phrases don't apply to you. Why? Because it's really not about her, it's about you. When you hold on to your N.U.T.s and consistently use the BetterMen Tools, you'll neither give her your balls, nor the opportunity to bust them.

If you're married, or considering marriage, the Tools will show you what it's going to take to be the married man you want to be. And for those of you who are divorced, separated, or about to commit to a long-term relationship, what you learn here will put you on the right path to being the man you want to be in your new relationships.

THE 8 BETTERMEN TOOLS

Nº. 1
SILENCE THE LITTLE BOY

Nº. 2
EXPRESS BUT DON'T DEFEND
YOUR FEELINGS

Nº. 3
COOPERATE WITHOUT
COMPROMISING YOUR N.U.T.s

Nº. 4
RUN THE SEX AND
ROMANCE DEPARTMENTS

Nº. 5
BE THE ROCK

Nº. 6
DON'T ARGUE

Nº. 7
LISTEN

Nº. 8
DEVELOP TRUSTING
RELATIONSHIPS WITH MEN

SILENCE THE LITTLE BOY

Who is the little boy we're talking about? You probably know him well, but here are some reminders: He's . . .

- the moody one who refuses to love or make love to his wife because she hurt his feelings.
- the one who expects his wife to read his mind and understand what he needs, even though he's done a terrible job of communicating those needs to her.
- the little boy who wants what he wants when he wants it and refuses to understand that choices have to be made, and that sometimes it doesn't work out the way he'd like.
- the one who expects his wife to satisfy all of his needs.
- the one who often leads the man to a quick fix, to seemingly more nurturing arms, or to divorce.

- the one who goes to battle with his wife every time he hears her complain—or thinks she's complaining—because he hears his mommy reprimanding him.
- the one who hasn't yet been initiated into manhood. He doesn't know how to be a man. He's stuck, as a little boy.

Recognize him? Most of us have that little boy in us. He's the one who didn't get the love, attention, guidance, mothering, fathering or discipline he should have gotten—or thinks he should have gotten—when he was a boy. He's also the real, wounded little boy who was abused or traumatized and never received the help he needed to heal and to grow up to be a healthy man.

INITIATING THE LITTLE BOY INTO MANHOOD

In tribal cultures, the little boy, through an initiation process led by the men of his community, is taught the ways of manhood and shown his place among the men. Through this rite of passage, the little boy is ceremonially "killed." Sometimes these rituals are so severe the boy himself is literally at risk of death.

When he returns to his village, the young man knows, as does his mother and the other villagers, that the boy has truly become a man. He knows what is expected of him and that there is no longer a place for the little boy in his life.

TOOLS IN USE

"I had a couple of issues in my previous marriage. My ex controlled my time with my daughter. I felt unduly criticized all the time. The worst part of it was that I just accepted these behaviors over time, not appreciating what was really happening—that a part of my soul was being eaten away each time I accepted the unacceptable.

That relationship ended and I eventually found a kind and caring woman who displayed none of these traits. However, since I was so conditioned by my ex, I fully expected the old behaviors to pop up with my new woman. And so, I braced myself for the eventual onslaught.

Surprise! The behaviors never surfaced, but I subconsciously acted as if they did. It took time for me to understand this and to react as a MAN to actual behaviors and actual events, rather than to what I perceived as my mate's "hidden meaning" or "intent." When I finally silenced the little boy, I championed the MAN! Silencing the little boy proved to be the critical turning point for me in my relationship. That change allowed me to honor what was most important to me and to not compromise my N.U.T.s."

—C.S.

In our culture, most boys do not experience this sort of initiation into manhood. Sure, some of us have teenage ceremonies that mark a boy's ascent into manhood. But they're just that, ceremonies and parties. They don't teach boys to be men. Instead, their fathers—who also were never initiated—teach them to be men in their image.

As a result, males in our society grow up without having a clear understanding of themselves as men, and they continue to act like needy little boys, especially when things aren't going well and when being a strong man is just what the situation requires.

Men who want to be happy as men, and successful in their relationships, need to be initiated into manhood and learn to silence their little boy. That can only happen by being with men and allowing them to share with you their wisdom—see Tool #8—Develop Trusting Relationships with Men.

For you, initiation will probably not take place in a short amount of time under the guidance of village elders. But it can happen, gradually, and only if you're committed to holding on to your N.U.T.s and bringing the BetterMen Tools to your relationships.

TIP!

The more you behave like the man you want to be, the more you silence the little boy.

TOOLS IN USE

"Last week I was on the verge of getting upset and angry because my needs were not met when I entered the door after my long day at work. I didn't get the kiss and hug I felt I deserved when I, the so-called King of the Household, came home.

I usually stomp off mad and upset, acting foolish and yes, childish. I know how immature I'm being, but I just can't seem to bolster enough faith in myself to overcome this little boy in me. But this time was different.

Instead of feeling alone and unwanted—and acting out accordingly, I was compassionate of my partner's mood and her very busy day. And for the very first time, I didn't give in to that little boy. At that moment, I finally saw a different side of me ... the man. That day, I was the man I wanted to be."

—L.K.

WHY SILENCE THE LITTLE BOY?

So why would you want to silence the little boy? For a guy on his own, with tons of cash and the freedom to spend it, there may seem to be little incentive. He can do what he wants, where and when he wants to. You know men like this. They're referred to as "that big kid," or the family friend who "refuses to grow up." He seems to have it all.

If you've been married a while, you may even envy that guy. But despite appearances, he doesn't have it all. In fact, there are a lot of those "big kids" who come to find that the one thing they really want, but don't have, is a close, intimate, long-term relationship with a woman. They don't know how to do that, and they certainly can't buy it with their money or secure it with their boyish charm. It can ultimately become a source of great pain for these men.

If you want to be successful in your long-term relationships, and you want to be the best husband you can be, you'll want to silence your little boy. Now, this is not about denying your pain or ignoring the healing that you may need to do. But as you do that work to heal, whether with the men or a counselor, you'll benefit by taking action to silence the little boy, and giving the man in you an opportunity to take charge. The more you act like the man, the more you'll heal the wounded little boy. **It's like being your own best father.**

To silence the little boy, you need to be able to recognize him and then develop skills to silence him, so that the man you want to be can take his rightful place on the throne. What follows are BetterMen Actions to help you recognize the little boy in you and to Silence the Little Boy.

WARNING!

Silencing the little boy refers to that hurt, needy little guy who's an obstacle to you becoming the best man you can be. But the little-boy energy that drives you to play balls-out, compete, wrestle, act stupid with your buddies and kids, is terrific and should be given every opportunity to find a place in your life. Don't silence that boy!

BETTERMEN ACTIONS

EMOTIONS + INSIGHT = FEELINGS

Emotions are what little boys have. Emotions are uninformed. They lack insight. They're knee-jerk reactions to experiences, interactions, words, people, etc.

Feelings are what the man can access. They're what develop when you take a look at your emotions and learn where they're coming from and the meanings they hold for you today, for the man. When a man knows how he feels, he can make his best decisions and be the best man he can be.

When all that's available are emotions, the little boy is in charge and that simply won't work for the man. Bring insight to your emotions and let the man run the show.

ANXIETY IS THE LITTLE BOY SCREAMING FOR HELP

Anxiety is not a feeling; it's a place to hide when you're afraid to acknowledge how you really feel. The little boy is anxious; the man can own his feelings. But being anxious is a good indication that there's work to do.

To help silence the little boy, ask yourself: If I weren't anxious right now, what would I be feeling? Would it be fear, sadness, loneliness, anger, shame or joy? Take the time to allow the true feeling to rise above the anxiety. When you have a handle on your feelings, you'll silence the little boy and give the man a chance to be a man.

DON'T EXPECT HER TO SATISFY ALL OF YOUR NEEDS

It's the surest way for the little boy to smother your wife, and slowly kill the relationship. You have needs that she cannot possibly satisfy, although a lot of loving women try. What happens is she gets frustrated because she can't satisfy all of your needs, and you get disappointed and resentful because you expect her to.

Silencing the little boy means recognizing that your wife is not supposed to be everything to you. It's time to reach out to other men—see Tool #8—Develop Trusting Relationships with Men and learn that what you really need—support and fathering—can only come from other men. Allow her to be your wife, and honor her by silencing the little boy.

THE BOY REACTS. THE MAN RESPONDS.

A good way to start figuring out the difference between the little boy and the man is to constantly be asking yourself this question: If I was the man I wanted to be right now, what would I do? Just taking that much time to consider your options will keep the boy from reacting, and give you the opportunity to respond like the man you want to be.

DEFENSIVENESS IS A RED FLAG

It's the little boy who says, "I didn't do it," "It wasn't me," or "It's not my fault." It's the little boy who's afraid to be wrong or to be punished. The man takes responsibility. Whatever it is, own it and clean it up. If you have to apologize, do it once and move on. If you want to be a man, and a good man at that, you've got to start acting like it.

STOP WHINING

Who wants to have sex with a whiner? And who wants to spend time with someone who complains and whines and acts like an annoying little boy? In Yiddish it's called kvetching. Whatever you call it, it's a relationship killer.

Complaining is just a bad habit you picked up as a child. It must have worked for you when you were a kid because you're still doing it. But guess what? It's not working anymore. It's time to silence the little boy by making the commitment to be a man who acts like a man and doesn't complain, whine or kvetch.

STOP BEING AFRAID OF YOUR WIFE

A lot of men are extremely uncomfortable when their wives are upset or simply not happy. They will sell themselves out—see chapter on N.U.T.s—just to change their wife's mood. If this is you, it's time to learn that, although this may have come from your past, it does not have to be a part of your present.

The little boy may have learned this behavior when he watched dad tip-toe around the house because he was afraid of mom. You may have learned to be afraid of women too. Your wife knows it and she doesn't like the power it gives her. She'd rather you Be the Rock—Tool #5. Silence the little boy by allowing her to have her own problems and to feel her own feelings without having to worry about how that makes you feel.

SILENCING THE LITTLE BOY ISN'T DENYING YOUR "INNER CHILD," IT'S FATHERING

Understanding the source of your pain is important. Counseling can help bring insight to your early childhood experiences. But getting into action and being the man you want to be will do more to heal that little boy than anything else. By focusing your attention on being the best man you can be, you reduce the energy going to that wounded little boy.

As you experience yourself being that man more and more, you'll find that your "inner child" will need less and less. Rather than deny the needs of the little boy, heal him by being your own best father.

MOODS BELONG TO THE LITTLE BOY

Men don't get moody. That's the little boy. It's the little boy who digs in his heels, holds a grudge, gets his feelings hurt, wants to strike back, gives the silent treatment, cancels plans to "show them," and on and on. The man acknowledges how he feels—perhaps after reaching out for a little help—and then acts accordingly.

When you feel yourself falling into one of your moods, know that you have the power to stop it, right in its tracks. Take a few minutes to think it through or call a friend. A simple effort like this can completely alter a moment, a day, a weekend or an entire vacation for you and those you care about. Silence the little boy by having power over his moods.

DON'T MEASURE YOUR PROGRESS BY HER REACTIONS

The little boy will see your wife upset and think he's done something wrong. Not necessarily. As you hold on to your N.U.T.s, she may not be pleased initially, or for a while. If you quit your efforts in response to her—assuming you're clear about your N.U.T.s and applying the Tools in a confident and caring way—you'll be giving your power away, again, and digging yourself into a deeper hole.

If you're not sure if you're doing a good job as a husband, check in with the men you trust. They'll tell you the truth. If they've quizzed you and feel confident that you've done a good job, trust them, have a little faith, and stay the course. Sometimes the hardest task for men is to hold on to those uncomfortable feelings long enough to see the fruits of their labor.

IN A N.U.T.SHELL

LET'S RECAP SILENCE THE LITTLE BOY:

- Identify the little boy in you, and commit to becoming the man.
- Remember that your wife is not your mother.
- Men who want to be happy as men, and successful in their relationships, need to be initiated into manhood and, with the help of other men, silence their little boy.
- Behave like the man you want to be, and the little boy will be silenced.
- The more you act like the man, the more you'll heal the wounded little boy.
- Silencing the little boy means keeping your emotions in check.
- Don't expect her—or anyone else—to satisfy all your needs or to read your mind.

- Allow your woman to have her own problems and to feel her own feelings without having to worry about how that makes you feel.

- The boy reacts from his emotions. The man brings insight and responds with mature feelings.

- The little boy has conditions, whereas the man holds on to his N.U.T.s.

- Be your own best father, and the little boy will grow up.

- Keep moving forward by using the BetterMen Actions.

THE 8 BETTERMEN TOOLS

Nº. 1
SILENCE THE LITTLE BOY

**Nº. 2
EXPRESS BUT DON'T DEFEND
YOUR FEELINGS**

Nº. 3
COOPERATE WITHOUT
COMPROMISING YOUR N.U.T.s

Nº. 4
RUN THE SEX AND
ROMANCE DEPARTMENTS

Nº. 5
BE THE ROCK

Nº. 6
DON'T ARGUE

Nº. 7
LISTEN

Nº. 8
DEVELOP TRUSTING
RELATIONSHIPS WITH MEN

TOOL Nº. 2

EXPRESS BUT DON'T DEFEND YOUR FEELINGS

Men are all screwed up about feelings. Not long ago, a man was a man if he kept his feelings to himself, you know, like John Wayne. Then it became popular for men to behave more like women and to express **all** of their feelings, all of the time, a la TV's Alan Alda. Neither approach is healthy for men, and neither makes for successful long-term relationships.

So does the answer lie somewhere in between the Duke and New Age man? Not quite.

A POWERFUL MAN KNOWS HOW HE FEELS

First, let's review your feelings. Remember those? They're the things which, if embraced as they are—without a bunch of social, familial, political and cultural influences piled on top—will guide you to making the best decisions for you. Acknowledging how you honestly feel will be your most effective tool in decision-making. When you're clear about how you feel, the solutions to your problems become clearer, too. Recognizing those feelings is important work for men who have been socialized in many ways to deny how they feel. **Being in your power** requires, first and foremost, knowing how you feel.

LET HER KNOW

In a long-term relationship, letting her know how you feel is critical. Many men have heard that from their women.

WARNING!

Don't be a bully. A man in his power doesn't manipulate, intimidate and interrogate to get his way or to prove his point. A man in his power is loving, accepting and compassionate. Express your feelings from this place, rather than being the resident bully.

TIP!

One of the best ways for men to figure out how they feel is to have a sounding board they can trust. Look for a male counselor, friend or mentor. The guy's got to be healthy and capable of hearing you, to help you figure out how you feel rather than imposing his fears, insecurities, judgments, etc., onto you. Also, his vision of manhood should mesh with your own.

The women are frustrated because they don't know how their men feel because their men are afraid to express their feelings. Why? Many of us were taught as boys to not honor our feelings—be tough, don't cry, etc. Some men were abused as boys and learned to stuff their feelings. For others, they've seen their feelings used against them, so they don't trust anymore. Now they're inexperienced or gun-shy when it comes to their own feelings. They don't know what to say, or they're afraid to say it.

Many men no longer trust themselves with their own feelings because they've seen themselves get sucked into arguments—or worse—whenever they've let down their guard. For these men, expressing their feelings has only led to more pain.

Your woman does need to know how you feel. When she doesn't, she feels less secure. And for women, security is a big deal. Security means feeling safe—safe in their homes, safe in their finances and safe in their relationships. When she knows how you feel, she's in a better position to care for you and the family, and to make choices that work for everyone.

After all, it's usually her job to manage all of that. She's usually the one trying to successfully juggle the wants and needs of the entire family. To do that, she needs to know how you feel. Do you like the idea she had, or not? Do you want to visit those relatives, or not? Are you angry with her and the kids or are you just worn out and being a jerk? She needs to know. Give her what she needs so she can do her job.

TOOLS IN USE

"My girlfriend and I had been together for about two years. She was at a point where she really wanted to get married and was putting a lot of pressure on me to make that commitment. When I would tell her I wasn't ready for marriage, I would find myself going through a very uncomfortable gauntlet of questions. Wasn't she good enough? When would I be ready? How long did I expect her to wait? Was I aware there were others who found her attractive and would jump at the chance? Etc.

The ending was always the same. She would not talk to me for a day or two and I would start to question myself. Was she going to leave me? Should I just marry her even though I didn't think I was ready? Should I just call it off now?

With the help of my men's team I was able to get clear on what I wanted. I wanted to get closer to her. I wanted to get married again. I loved her and wanted us to stay together. But I wasn't ready to get married, yet. I also knew the "high pressure" discussions we were having pushed me further away from her.

So it became clear that I had to let her know exactly how I felt—without defending my feelings. I told her these exact things. Since then we have become closer. We no longer have the "high pressure" discussions and we have actually started to have talks about how things would be if we were to move in together.

Being afraid to come to terms with my feelings—and keeping her in the dark—didn't work for either of us. Having the clarity and the courage to tell her how I felt—and knowing I would not defend my feelings or argue about them— actually made things better, a lot better."

—I.S.

When you learn to express your feelings without defending them, you'll be giving her what she needs, strengthening your relationship, and feeling much more like the best man you can be. Expressing your feelings will also help you avoid the anger, stress, resentment, depression—and a host of other undesirable emotional and physical outcomes—that come with stuffing them.

DON'T DILUTE YOUR MESSAGE

Now, why would you defend your feelings? Well, if you're unsure of your feelings or you haven't worked those muscles in a while, you may feel that simply stating your feelings is insufficient. Feeling insecure about yourself, you

TIP!

Here are a few examples of what it may sound like for you to express your feelings without defending them:

- I love that.
- That makes me really angry.
- I'm really frustrated when the kids behave that way.
- I'm sorry I hurt you.
- I'm scared.
- When you do that thing, I fall in love with you all over again.
- I'm not upset, I'm just really tired. Can we talk about this tomorrow?
- I like both colors (of paint, carpet, drapes, etc.) and I trust you to make our house look great.

WARNING!

When it's time to express your feelings, DON'T have any expectations of her reaction. When you act like the man you want to be, her reactions will, eventually, be unlike anything you've ever seen from her. Some men see an immediate change in their woman's response.

Remember, they respond to us. If you're the best man you can be, the response you'll receive—eventually—will be good. It may take some time for her to trust this new you, but have faith in this process and in your ability to let her know how you feel without too much explanation. She'll get it, and she'll appreciate it.

may find yourself saying more and more until you get the response you're looking for from her. You may be expecting her sympathy or her approval. But the truth is, the more you say, the more you're diluting your message and the closer you're getting to engaging in a discussion **about** your feelings rather than effectively communicating **what** you are feeling.

Logic can be defended. If you're having a discussion about politics, religion or sports, you can defend your position, relying on the day's headlines, history or statistics to support your position. If you can have those sorts of discussions with your woman, great! But when it comes to your feelings, there is nothing to defend. How you feel is how you feel. And the same is true for her. So be a good listener for her. See Tool #7—Listen.

IT'S TEST TIME

Now, why would a woman question you about how you feel? In some cases, she may be testing you to see just how committed you are to those feelings. In other cases, she's doing it because she doesn't like how you feel, she doesn't like how your reaction makes **her** feel, or she's not happy about how the way you feel may affect some choices you'll make—choices that could affect her or your family. **She may want you to change how you feel so it makes her feel better.** (By the way, men do the same thing with their women.)

She'll do this by questioning you about your feelings, and once you engage in the process of defending your feelings, you're a goner. You've just crossed into territory that is beyond your ability to navigate. You may be heading for an argument. Women naturally talk about their feelings. Unless they've done some work developing these particular skills, most men get lost in these types of discussions.

For instance, let's say she threw away the newspaper today before you had a chance to read it. And let's say that you've asked her several times not to do that, even though she likes to toss all of the papers away on recycling day. You say to her this time: "It really upsets me when you do that."

TOOLS IN USE

"Intuitively, I knew that I had to do something different when my wife and I would have a fight. I would see the pattern and I would say to myself "OK, I see her festering, how can I defuse this?" Not having the Tools sent me down the same path that I had gone down for the last 20-plus years. That path included disagreement, confrontation, yelling, anger, and then seclusion. Then, because she never breaks the ice, I would always be the one to acquiesce and initiate the path to "making up."

Now when we have a disagreement, I listen attentively and when I understand her position, I tell her that I understand. I will not ramp-up the tone when she does. I have managed to integrate the "express but don't defend my feelings" mantra into my psyche. It has helped tremendously. If she chooses to escalate and continue the ramp-up, I simply say, "I have heard enough" and walk away. She has begun to get that I will not be brow-beaten.

What I have found by making these few changes is that I am feeling better about who I am. I am feeling more respected by my wife. I am seeing us argue less and with considerably less residual ill feelings. I feel more in charge of my feelings and I find my wife asking me things more now and waiting for an answer, instead of knowing that I will agree with her. For the first time in our relationship, I am feeling the balance of power tipping to equilibrium."

— D.L.

WARNING!

"I feel angry . . . cuz you're a bitch" is not an effective execution of expressing without defending your feelings. Actually, it's just another attack disguised as an "I statement."

Try this: "I don't want to be with you when you act that way."

Now, she's not going to like that you're upset. She may even, in that moment, realize that she screwed up, but may not be willing or capable of acknowledging it. Instead, she may say, "Geez, you don't have to get so angry about it. Why are you so angry?"

Do you really have to explain? Doesn't she already know? So instead of answering that question and defending your feelings by saying something like "I've asked you countless times. Why can't you listen?" you're better off just saying, "You know how I feel about this." She's perfectly capable of figuring out a solution.

There's simply nothing to be gained by getting into an argument. You've made your point in the clearest, most concise way, without attacking her or arguing with her about your feelings or her feelings. You can now let it go and relax. You've done your job. It may not feel good to you at the time, but you'll see it works much better than any alternative, from saying nothing, quashing your feelings and holding resentment, to arguing with her and possibly saying something you'll regret.

What follows are BetterMen Actions for the Tool: Express But Don't Defend Your Feelings. These are some recommended ways for you to practice being the best man you can be by getting clear about your feelings and then sharing them with your woman in a way that best supports her, your relationship, and your N.U.T.s.

BETTERMEN ACTIONS

READ TOOL #8—DEVELOP TRUSTING RELATIONSHIPS WITH MEN

Before you can deliver the goods, you'll need to know what the goods are. There's no better way to get clear about how we feel than by getting the support of other men. For this and all of the other Tools, having men in your life is always a good place to start.

START WITH "I"

Although it's not a guarantee for effectiveness, it is a good place to start. If you're wanting to tell her how you feel, you won't be getting your message across if you say hurtful things like, "What the hell are you doing?" or "What are you, stupid?" Telling her how you feel would sound more like, "I feel sad when you treat yourself that way," or "I would be a happy guy if you'd ask for my help when you needed something like this (you fill in the blank) done for you."

IF YOU'RE NOT SURE—BUY YOURSELF SOME TIME

Imagine you're on your neighborhood bomb squad. You've got the wire cutters in your hand, sweat's dripping down your face, the digital display reads five minutes—and counting—and you can't remember whether it's red then black, or black then red.

If you find yourself in this sweaty place with your woman, your best bet is to either get help—if available—or "take five" and allow yourself to get into a clearer frame of mind. Take a time-out from the situation. Perhaps then you'll be able to see the best course of action. The worst thing you could do is to cut the wrong wire. Got the picture?

If you're feeling on the spot, pressured to share a thought or feeling but not confident you know where you stand, it's OK to wait. It's fine to say, "Let me think about it," or " Let's talk more tomorrow."

You've now given yourself time to either think about it on your own, or pick up the phone and call a man you trust. A quick conversation with a man you trust is sometimes all you need to get clear about the most unclear of situations. But remember to get back to her. Don't make her track you down. This isn't a trick to avoid having to express your feelings. It's a legitimate method to insure that what you say is truly what you mean, how you feel.

WHEN YOU'RE DONE, LISTEN

Remember that you're not there to argue—see Tool #6—Don't Argue. You simply want her to know how you feel. Be proud of yourself for doing a good job. Enjoy the moment, even if she's having a tough time hearing what you have to say.

Eventually, this healthier form of communication will make a huge difference in how you feel as a man in your relationship. If you have a committed and loving mate, she'll appreciate the change as well. Now listen to her and be interested in how she feels. See Tool #7—Listen.

FORGET YOUR PAST. BE YOUR BEST TODAY!

Whether it's your current wife or girlfriend, or a former lover, forget what's happened in the past—the pain, the arguments, the misunderstandings. Time to let it all go. Don't let your past hurts keep you from being the best man you can be today.

Letting go means forgiving, forgetting and surrendering your need to be right. We all make mistakes. The question you need to answer is whether it's more important for you to be "right," or to be in a loving relationship.

DON'T BEAT HER UP

Hitting her is unacceptable at anytime, for any reason. What we're talking about here is equally unacceptable—beating her up verbally. It's hurtful, unproductive and it'll destroy what you want most.

Women oftentimes know when they've screwed up. Many, especially those who were ridiculed as kids or had authoritarian parents, are beating themselves up before you can even get out your first reprimanding word. Your job is to not pile on.

It may be hard to restrain yourself in the heat of the moment—when you want to be the one to let her know how wrong you think she is. But holding your fire is the kindest and most effective approach. Telling her how you feel without reprimanding her is all you need to do. You do your job right and she'll find a way to let you know how well you handled the situation—and her.

EXPRESSING YOUR FEELINGS NEVER INCLUDES NAME-CALLING

Calling her a hurtful name while you're upset, or at any time, really, is simply wrong. It hurts her and eats away at your relationship. What you want is to get closer. Calling her names will guarantee that intimacy never takes place.

If all that comes to mind are words like *bitch*, *c*nt*, and *whore*, or phrases like, "you're just like your mother," "you're so stupid," or "I can't stand you," leave the room and cool off. It's abusive behavior and it's a red flag. Get some help before you destroy everything that truly means something to you, like your marriage and your family.

DON'T MAKE IT ABOUT HER

You may have been affected by something she did or said. But those strong feelings you're experiencing may actually have nothing to do with her. What's happened is that her behavior or her words have triggered feelings in you. They are your feelings and they're often connected to events that took place a long time ago, way before she came on the scene.

So, beyond expressing how you feel about what she did or said, don't dwell on it. Put the emphasis on how it feels for you and leave it at that. Next, seek some help to find out what those deeper feelings are all about. The more you understand where they are coming from, the better you'll understand where you are coming from.

GIVE YOURSELVES SOME TIME TO ADJUST

You may have a difficult time learning to express your feelings without defending them. She may need some time to get used to this change in her man. Don't expect this new behavior to work like a charm from the start, or to be instantly integrated into your relationship. It takes practice and patience; the results will follow.

TAKE A N.A.P.

It's easy to focus on our negative behaviors when we're trying to make changes in our lives. But it's so important to let her know the positive feelings you have about her, how supportive she's been, how patient she is with the kids, etc. Express your loving, happy and supportive feelings every chance you get.

And here's an acronym that may help you remember to take care of her: N.A.P.: Notice, Acknowledge and Praise. It means pay attention to what she's doing, see it for the positive behavior that it is, and make sure she knows how much you appreciate her.

Although many men have never seen this technique applied by their old-school dads, it really does work. So be sure to N.A.P. often. As you apply the Tools and get to know your woman's needs, you'll find how effective a N.A.P. can be.

LEARN TO KNOW WHEN NOT TO EXPRESS YOUR FEELINGS

After you review all of the Tools, you'll understand there are times when it's best not to share certain feelings with her. Some of those feelings need to be taken to the men. For instance, recall an instance when you were extremely angry with her. Do you remember the ugly, awful, mean, toxic thoughts that went through your mind—at the speed of light? If you shared them with her, how long do you think it would take for her to forgive and forget? Exactly. A long time, if ever.

But these thoughts, feelings and words are a part of you. They need to be expressed so you can make sense of them. That's why Develop Trusting Relationships with Men—Tool #8—and asking them for support is so important. Not expressing them with her, but having a safe place to unload and to learn, will help you to Be the Rock—Tool #5—for her. Likewise, when you're battling with Tool #1—Silence the Little Boy—bringing to the men what you should not share with her will help you to be the man you want to be, instead of the needy little boy. You'll find that getting clear with the men, whether with a men's group, counselor or friend, will help you to learn what to share and when.

This is not about keeping secrets. It's really about taking care of her and you. There are some things she doesn't need to know. And there are some things you shouldn't burden her with, things best shared with the men.

SHOW HER HOW YOU FEEL

Sometimes no words are necessary. When she's being supportive, when she adjusts to your new behaviors in ways you appreciate, and when she makes positive changes for herself that you admire, it's time to show her how you feel. Make an extra effort around the house, bring home something that has special meaning for her, take her out on the town, or simply give her a big wet one. It may be in a card, with some flowers, or demonstrated by some heroic effort to get something finally fixed or cleaned up around the house. In other words, don't let any good deed on her part go unappreciated.

IN A N.U.T.SHELL

LET'S RECAP EXPRESS BUT DON'T DEFEND YOUR FEELINGS:

- Being clear about how you feel is your most effective tool in decision making.

- Look for a male counselor, friend or mentor to help you figure out how you feel.

- It's your job to let her know how you feel.

- Don't be a bully.

- Expressing your feelings eliminates the anger, stress, resentment and depression that come with stuffing them.

- Saying too much will have you engaging in a discussion about your feelings—and defending them—rather than effectively communicating what you are feeling.

- When it comes to your feelings, there is nothing to defend. How you feel is how you feel. And the same is true for her.

- Be prepared for the inevitable tests. She'll want to know whether you're really committed to these new N.U.T.s and Tools.

- N.A.P. — Notice, Acknowledge and Praise — whenever possible.

- Show her how you feel.

- There are some things she doesn't need to know about. Get some support and find out what you don't need to share.

- Keep moving forward by using the BetterMen Actions.

THE 8 BETTERMEN TOOLS

Nº. 1
SILENCE THE LITTLE BOY

Nº. 2
EXPRESS BUT DON'T DEFEND
YOUR FEELINGS

**Nº. 3
COOPERATE WITHOUT
COMPROMISING YOUR N.U.T.s**

Nº. 4
RUN THE SEX AND
ROMANCE DEPARTMENTS

Nº. 5
BE THE ROCK

Nº. 6
DON'T ARGUE

Nº. 7
LISTEN

Nº. 8
DEVELOP TRUSTING
RELATIONSHIPS WITH MEN

COOPERATE WITHOUT COMPROMISING YOUR N.U.T.s

Is this even possible? "There's no pleasing that woman," you say? Well, it's not your job to make her happy—that's up to her. But you can be a better partner. You can help her out a bit more in taking care of you and your family. You can show some enthusiasm for her restaurant suggestion, how to spend the day or when to visit the in-laws. And you can get your butt out of the recliner to do some of those things she'd appreciate being done, **without compromising your N.U.T.s**, and without needing her acknowledgment or praise for doing it.

WARNING!

Is your resistance to cooperate with her about her? Ask yourself this question: Would I have a problem cooperating right now if someone other than my wife asked me to do the same thing? If the answer is no, it's time to ask for help, to gain some insight, or simply to make a new choice.

So many N.U.T.-less men—men without Non-negotiable, Unalterable Terms—make an issue of those honey-do's—a term that has got to go. It represents the way men without their N.U.T.s have characterized the things they'll reluctantly do for their wives despite their growing sense of emasculation, resentment, rage and despair. In other words, they'll do it, but they won't be happy about it. As a result, they act out in ways to let her know they're unhappy, only causing further damage to their relationships.

Instead, take responsibility, honor your commitments and follow through. That's how a man with integrity would handle it. Or would you prefer spending your life doing honey-do's?

WHY WE DON'T COOPERATE

Some men are resistant to cooperating with their women because they're angry and it's their way of getting even. For instance, he refuses to make the bed because "that's her job." The truth is, he's either angry with her because their sex life sucks, he feels abandoned by her, or some other real issue that hasn't been addressed properly. Remember the "conditions" discussed earlier?

Again, this is what passive-aggressive behavior looks like. There's a much better way of being the best husband you can be while still being a man who holds on to his N.U.T.s.

TIP!

Ask yourself this question: if you don't cooperate with her, help her, support her and otherwise take care of her, who will? Do you really want to find out? Gather your N.U.T.s and get to work!

If you want to see your relationship improve, to have the kind of home environment that you'd always hoped for, and to be a happy and married man, it's time for you to make a commitment. Once you've got a hold of your N.U.T.s—you might want to reread the chapter on N.U.T.s so you're clear about the differences between terms and conditions—it's time to commit to being a loving, supportive and cooperative husband. It's time to Silence the Little Boy—see Tool #1— and act like the man and husband you want to be.

Why wouldn't you want to cooperate with her? What do you get out of being stubborn? Does it make you feel better in the long run? Does it improve your sex life? Does it encourage closeness between the two of you? Does it make for a home you love to return to after a hard day at work? Does it support the two of you to be the best parents

TOOLS IN USE

"I was really put to the test with respect to "cooperate without compromising your N.U.T.s." My stepson decided on short notice to get married—on my anniversary date—to a girl who did not like me and my wife, and all other family members. In response to this and other equally inconsiderate behaviors, I was determined not to go to his wedding.

However, my wife wanted to go to her son's wedding, and needed my support. So, on the advice of other men, I switched the focus of the weekend from "their wedding" to "our anniversary." Instead of a miserable few hours, I created a three-day weekend celebrating our anniversary, with a pit stop at a wedding. A bed-and-breakfast hotel, private mineral spring hot tubs, massages, fine meals, and, of course, shopping because my wife loves to shop! Seventy-two hours of fun.

I kept my N.U.T.s, I cooperated with her, I ran the sex and romance departments and I was the rock, with a little help from the men. It works."

— G.I.

you can be for your kids? The answer to all of these questions is probably "no." So why continue behaving this way by not cooperating?

So, stop complaining about trivial requests. Stop acting like a little boy. If she wants you to feed the animals, feed the animals. If the trash needs go out, do it promptly. If she wants you to stop your weekly men's group because she really wants you home . . . whoa! That's important to you. It's a non-negotiable. It's not up for discussion. No need to argue about it. It's one of your N.U.T.s. She may be upset with you for the moment. But if you're consistent with your N.U.T.s and consistent with cooperating, you will be a man she can respect and appreciate.

WARNING!

Make sure you spend sufficient time with your family. If your weekly poker night is just one of the five nights per week you're gone, it may be time to re-examine your commitment to being the best husband and father you can be.

Chances are, there are unexamined feelings keeping you away from home. It's in your best interest, and the best interest of your family, to have the courage to address and resolve these issues.

This may also be an opportunity to examine the balance in your life between work, family and other interests.

TOOLS IN USE

"My wife phoned me at work and relayed a story to me about a salesman who came to the door selling magazines. I know she has a difficult time saying no to peddlers who come to our door. I have told her a million times, if she wants to buy magazines, great, but I will pay for them through the business. So just let me know and I will submit the subscription.

She continued the story telling me how the salesman kept adding fees. She was clearly being taken advantage of. I could feel my blood pressure steadily rising and my patience for her and her story nearing an end. As I began to get pissed off, I caught myself and took a deep breath and told her I'd see her when I got home.

When I walked in the door, she was resting in bed after her "long day." Instead of being pissed off, I took a different approach. I walked up to her, gave her a hug and told her I understood that she had a bad day. There was no need to mention the magazines. She knew.

I didn't argue with her. And this time I didn't even have to express my feelings about what had happened. Instead, I just cared about her. Although I'd prefer if she'd let me expense subscriptions through the business, I can't say it's a N.U.T. of mine. It's not that important. So instead, I just cooperated with her. It totally defused my anxiety, and I can only hope that she'll think twice before buying magazines from door-to-door salesmen again."

— E.L.

Can you see how, if you hold on to your N.U.T.s, you can cooperate with her without feeling resentment? Can you imagine doing things for her and supporting her and feeling great about it?

The best course of action regarding this Tool is to take action. What follows are BetterMen Actions for the Tool: Cooperate Without Compromising Your N.U.T.s. These are some recommended ways for you to practice being the best man you can be and demonstrating your commitment to the relationship.

BETTERMEN ACTIONS

FOR ONE WEEK, PUT HER FIRST

Without compromising your N.U.T.s, do whatever she asks, when she asks it. Think of things to make her life easier. Find ways to give her a break. Stop procrastinating and finish that project; clean the garage, help with the kids at bath time, etc. The possibilities are endless.

See how you feel when the week is up. See how she responds. See if you can identify your own reasons for recommitting to another week of the same, and then do it. This could get to be a habit!

THINK YOU'RE LAZY? THINK AGAIN

"Lazy" is often a convenient place for men to hide out. It's like being confused or bored. It's easy for us to blame our inaction on these "stuck" states of being. These are just places you can hang out in so you don't have to make a decision or take responsibility. Is that the best man, husband and father you can be?

Make this commitment: When you recognize you're being lazy, confused or bored, do something different. Get into action! These may be the best times for you to find a way to cooperate with her and challenge yourself to be a better man. You may find that this BetterMen Action applies to other areas of your life. Think about it. How would your life and relationships change for the better if you simply took full responsibility?

NOT SURE IF YOU'RE BEING ASKED TO COMPROMISE YOUR N.U.T.s?

OK, that's fine. Now's a great time to review the work you've done to identify your N.U.T.s. It's impossible to execute this Tool properly without being clear about your N.U.T.s. If you don't know your N.U.T.s, you'll always be in doubt and the resentment will build. If reviewing your N.U.T.s on your own doesn't help, call a man you trust. Go over things with him and ask for help. Again, Tool #8— Develop Trusting Relationships with Men—is indispensable in your efforts to be the best husband you can be.

MAKE A LIST

Take some time to think about the things she's asked you to do in the past, when you've either procrastinated, ignored her completely, or did a lousy or incomplete job. Write them all down. Now, check this list against your N.U.T.s. Are there any obvious conflicts? Eliminate those requests that would have you compromising your N.U.T.s. Is there anything keeping you from acting on this list now? If so, bring it to the men you trust and find out what your feelings are about these issues. Let the men help you to get unstuck.

If the list isn't a problem, commit to taking action today to start knocking the items off one-by-one. This would also be a great opportunity to ask a man to hold you accountable to the commitment. See Tool #8— Develop Trusting Relationships with Men. When you share your commitment with another good man, and ask him to hold you accountable, the likelihood of you honoring that commitment increases exponentially.

HAVE YOU SILENCED THE LITTLE BOY?

If anything like, "I don't want to," "She doesn't deserve it," or "When was the last time she did what I wanted?" is rattling around in your head, you'll first need to silence that little boy before you'll be available to cooperate with her. You're allowing that needy and powerful little guy to screw up your relationship.

Concentrate on Tool #1—Silence the Little Boy—and see how the little boy in you is making it difficult for you to cooperate with her without compromising your N.U.T.s.

BE A NICE GUY

Have you forgotten how to be a nice guy? Some men are so disconnected from their women—because they've been angry, frustrated or unhappy for so long—they can't even muster a little compassion, a kiss, or a sweet note of appreciation left on the counter. If this is the man you've become, make a change.

Don't waste more time justifying, rationalizing, judging or blaming. Don't wait for her to change. Be nice, helpful and responsive. Maybe you're not "in love" with her at the moment. But start being the man you want to be and you may be surprised by the changes you see in her . . . and you.

IN A N.U.T.SHELL

LET'S RECAP COOPERATE WITHOUT COMPROMISING YOUR N.U.T.s:

- Mastering this tool requires you to be clear about your N.U.T.s.

- Cooperating means getting your butt out of the recliner and doing those things she'd appreciate being done, without compromising your N.U.T.s, and without needing her acknowledgment or praise for doing it.

- Men resist cooperating when they're angry, allowing their little boys to dig in their heels. And, not cooperating will not improve your sex life.

- When you recognize you're being lazy, confused or bored, do something about it. Get into action.

- Take responsibility, honor your commitments and follow through. That's the approach of a man with integrity.

- Commit to being a loving, supportive and cooperative husband.

- If you're in doubt as to whether you're being asked to compromise your N.U.T.s, call the men and ask for help.
- If you want to have the kind of home environment you'd always hoped for, make a commitment to consistently use this Tool.
- Don't wait for her to change. Just be a nice guy.
- Keep moving forward by using the BetterMen Actions.

THE 8 BETTERMEN TOOLS

Nº. 1
SILENCE THE LITTLE BOY

Nº. 2
EXPRESS BUT DON'T DEFEND
YOUR FEELINGS

Nº. 3
COOPERATE WITHOUT
COMPROMISING YOUR N.U.T.s

Nº. 4
RUN THE SEX AND
ROMANCE DEPARTMENTS

Nº. 5
BE THE ROCK

Nº. 6
DON'T ARGUE

Nº. 7
LISTEN

Nº. 8
DEVELOP TRUSTING
RELATIONSHIPS WITH MEN

RUN THE SEX AND ROMANCE DEPARTMENTS

For the most part, women need to feel intimacy to want to have sex. Men need to have the sex to feel the intimacy. So, is this an impossible situation? Not really. If you take care of the romance, she'll feel the love. When she feels the love, she'll give you the sign. When she gives you the sign, it's all up to you. If you do your job, you'll both feel the closeness. That's it in a nutshell.

The only problem is that men don't always take care of the "business" of romance. That's what this Tool is all about.

When you first met, sex and romance probably came very easily to both of you. The ground rules were set, and you both wanted to do it all the time. So what happened?

It's easy to blame it on marriage, her, the kids, busy schedules, etc. These factors are real, and they definitely make for a greater challenge. But in the end, they're just excuses. And are excuses what you want your life to be about? If you were the man you wanted to be, would you settle for less?

YOU HOLD THE POWER TO IMPROVE YOUR SEX LIFE

It's time for you to see what incredible power you have to keep your sex life vital, to have a frequency to your liking (although it may not always live up to your fantasies), and to build the intimacy you both want in your relationship.

WARNING!

Close all "back doors" to infidelity, old girlfriends and pornography!

If you really want to turn your relationship around and take charge of the sex and romance, you must close the back doors. Back doors allow you to "sneak out" and compromise on your commitments. They're distractions and energy drains. Any energy going out the back door is energy that's not going into your relationship.

Don't expect the tide to turn until you make a real commitment and install a deadbolt on that back door.

TOOLS IN USE

"When I was 24 I married my first wife. We were both virgins on our wedding night. I was really horny but ignorant about being a sexual man. At the time I did not have anyone to confide in, including my wife. So sex became a place of frustration, failure and embarrassment.

Twenty-six years later, my third wife—as our marriage was ending—said, for her having sex with me was like "being with a boy, not a man." During those 26 years I continued to have no one I trusted to confide in about the deep pain I felt around my sex life. I actually thought the problem was one of technique and so I eagerly pored over magazine articles like "10 Things That Will Drive Her Wild."

Two years later I joined a men's group. For the first time, I began to talk about what I had never wanted anyone to know about me. I was finally able to identify the feeling and attitude of being a man. Having men to trust and confide in has made all the difference. I learned how to show up with my woman in the same way that I was showing up in business. I found that the confident and powerful attitude that had helped make me a success in my career was exactly what she wanted to experience of me sexually.

Today, no woman will ever say that having sex with me is like 'being made love to by a boy, and not a man.' Not any more!"

—S.K.

TIP!

Master Tool #3—Cooperate Without Compromising Your N.U.T.s. Cooperate with her and you'll find that running the sex and romance departments will get a whole lot easier. She needs the intimacy in order to want the sex. She'll feel the intimacy more when she gets what she needs, when she feels that you care about her.

Cooperating with her and handling what she wants you to handle—without compromising your N.U.T.s—is an important way for you to show her you care, and to be the kind of man she wants to do!

First, we need to get clear about why this is important to you. First, you enjoy sex, yes? And you also want to feel close to her, for it to feel effortless to be with her, to be partners, to have fun with her, and to feel like you're on the same team, like a couple. In your wife's magazines, they call this "intimacy."

Some men have a hard time with this word—intimacy. It's been associated over the years with everything women want from men and everything men are supposedly incapable of giving to them—unless they, too, behave like women.

Being intimate is laughing together, sitting quietly, or reading together. Intimacy is holding hands on a walk, a movie date, a massage, holding her while she's crying, and falling asleep in front of the fireplace together. Intimacy is that, and hundreds of other things. It's whatever the two of you do that make you glad you're with each other. Intimacy comes from you taking the time to let her know what she means to you. And to do that, Romeo, it takes a little romance.

ROMANCE HER

Romance. This is the stuff you do to let her know you love her, to let her know you care, to let her know she's sexy, and to let her know you want to bang her brains out.

TIP!

Be the man your wife would like to have an affair with.

Maybe it's been a while since you've had sex, gone out on a date, or spent a night at a secluded hotel. If you find yourself thinking about the cute kindergarten teacher at your kid's school, or fantasizing about the hot cashier at the local market, your wife may be doing her own browsing.

The solution? Act like that stud she's dreaming about. Be unpredictable. Get off your butt. Be creative. Plan a getaway and only tell her what clothing she'll need to bring. Take her to a new restaurant. Set up the babysitter yourself and whisk her away to a concert of her favorite rock legends. Be that man and let her live her fantasy, instead of just dreaming about it.

After a while, married men come to believe that, even though they've forgotten about the romance, they should still have the same sex lives as when they were dating. It doesn't work that way. Or, at least, it doesn't work very well.

YOU KNOW WHAT SEX IS, RIGHT?

Sex. This is the stuff you do with each other you don't want the kids to see. Do you really need this defined? Well, maybe some of you do. It's touching, massaging, role-playing, foreplay, the actual "act" in all its glory and its many positions, and making sure she's as satisfied as you know she can be when you've done your best. That's sex.

Does that define your recent experiences with your wife? If not, read on, good man.

DAMN THAT LITTLE BOY!

The most common and lethal barrier to being the best husband and lover you can be is allowing the little boy to run the show. Mastering Tool #1—Silence the Little Boy—is

> Maybe nobody told you, but to keep the marriage strong and the sex great, the romance must continue, forever. And that's *your* job.

TIP!

Cherish and Protect

That's our job, to cherish and protect our women. They want to feel special, cared for and loved. And they want to feel safe. Holding on to your N.U.T.s and using the Tools will help you to cherish and protect your woman.

a crucial first step to becoming the CEO of the sex and romance departments. Here's a typical scenario demonstrating how the little boy shows up in some relationships. See if any of this sounds familiar:

You haven't had sex for a while—maybe a few days, maybe a couple weeks. You've been working hard or have been away. She's been sick or having her period. The kids have kept you up for one reason or another. The days turn into weeks, the couple of weeks turn into a month. There's tension because you're not getting what you want—of course, you're not doing what you need to do to make it happen, either.

She's feeling the tension as well. Resentment builds. What the hell, you might as well jerk-off or look at porn to get what your wife is "clearly unwilling" to provide. Resentment grows. You realize one day that she's not as attractive as she used to be. Maybe you notice her few extra pounds or you're annoyed by some of the things she says or does. You find yourself thinking more and more about seeking outside action. You eventually become resigned to the fact that you won't be getting it anymore, or as regularly, as you once did. You feel stuck and you're pissed off.

Of course, she's completely unaware of the little boy who's been screaming in your head. When it does come out—and eventually it will—it will be poorly timed, guaranteed. And how it comes out will be so tainted with resentment, it'll take an archeologist to dig deep enough to get to the real truth.

Any of this strike a chord? This is the painful result of allowing the little boy, that moody, needy and afraid little guy, to govern how you—the man—show up in your marriage around sex and romance. It's time to silence that little

WARNING!

Fear of rejection belongs to your little boy. Silence him by acting like the man, the kind of man your woman wants in her bed.

She's not your mother. She's your partner, your wife. Stop seeking her approval and stop allowing yourself to be paralyzed by her "rejections."

This time she may not be into it. But next time she probably will be. Be the man who can be confident, considerate, romantic and persistent. That man, the man in his power, doesn't mistake inopportune timing for personal rejection.

boy and start assuming your role as the man of the house, the man in your marriage, the man in your sex life."

How do you do that? Get into action. You may be afraid of rejection, but there are no short cuts here. You have to start by taking the reins. And if she says "no," don't act like the little boy and pout, get angry, or shut down emotion-

TOOLS IN USE

"I could see it going down the same bad path. We hadn't had sex for a couple of weeks. You know, kids, period, work, and being tired. I could feel myself getting annoyed and then pissed at her for not initiating. I always seem to be the one who initiates.

But then I started to remember the things I had heard in my men's group a hundred times: To run the sex and romance department you have to silence the little boy. I suppose I had heard it so many times from the men that it was finally occurring to me when I needed it most, in the moment.

Despite the fear of being rejected because I might have picked a "bad time," I found her in the kitchen, hugged her hard, looked her in the eye and—while working my hand down to her zone—said, "I'll see you upstairs in two minutes." And I did!

I'm always forgetting I have the power to turn these "droughts" around. Now my challenge is to minimize the number of these dry spells because I want sex more often, and it's about time that I not let my moods push her away."

—S.A.

ally. Keep at it. It may be difficult for you at first, but in time, you'll find your groove.

What follows is a long list of BetterMen Actions for the Tool: Run The Sex and Romance Departments. Don't get intimidated by the number of suggestions. Find one that feels right to you, and do it. Once you get started—and you experience the results—you'll have the motivation you need to keep it going.

WARNING!

Don't get complacent. Once you execute one or more of these BetterMen Actions, you'll probably find that your wife is happier and your relationship's gotten a bit more intimate. This is no time to rest on your laurels. Revisit the BetterMen Actions listed below and keep doing your job.

So maybe it's not as easy as it was during the honeymoon period. But if you're committed to your relationship and you're willing to be the best husband you can be, you may find yourselves on a second honeymoon. Really, this stuff works. Trust the men.

BETTERMEN ACTIONS

ASK FOR HELP

Are you feeling completely inadequate, unable to take the initiative to make plans for the two of you? Chill. You're not alone. The best suggestion we have is for you to ask for help. Ask other men—Tool #8—Develop Trusting Relationships with Men. Approach a man you respect, someone you think has a good relationship with his wife, and ask his advice. He'll gladly help you out.

When you ask someone for help, you're giving him the opportunity to be of service, and that's a gift. The important thing for you to remember is that this action you're taking is an important start. Baby steps, good buddy. You'll get there.

REVIVE THE GOLDEN OLDIES

Think back to the days when you did whatever it took to make her yours. Remember what really turned her on? Rather than trying to figure out why you haven't done that for so long, just go ahead and set it up. Yeah, it may be a little tougher these days, what with the kids, responsibilities, work and all. But who else is going to take care of it?

Make that first big effort and keep the momentum going. Just do it for her without expecting anything in return. Don't worry, you'll be taken care of in time.

DO "IT" NOW AND DO IT YOUR WAY

Have sex now. Put down this book, find her and carry her into the bedroom, or the kitchen, or the den, or wherever you can reach before your back goes out. Once you're there, do a really good job. Be sensitive to her needs, but you also want to push the envelope, get unpredictable, risk trying something new. That ought to put a smile on her face, and yours too!

THE BEST TIME TO HAVE SEX IS WHEN YOU WANT TO GIVE

When you care about her and make this time about her and for her, you're in a giving mood. This is good. Coming from this selfless place will do wonders for her and for your relationship. Getting yourself into this giving mindset may simply mean a shift in your attitude. This attitude adjustment might require you to Silence the Little Boy—Tool #1. Read it again.

RESERVE SOME TIME FOR HER

Before the day is through, make a reservation at her favorite restaurant. If you need to, arrange for childcare. If there are any other potential conflicts, think them through and make the necessary calls. All of this will take you just a few minutes.

Most importantly, when you actually go out, do your best to make the evening about her. Listen to her—Tool #7. See what she wants to talk about. Make the occasion special for her. Of course, there are opportunities throughout the night to add extra touches. But even if it's a simple outing, she'll appreciate the time you spent planning it.

WHISK HER AWAY

Take her away for the weekend. There are hotels, spas and bed-and-breakfasts everywhere. You can find them all over the web. A buddy might know of the perfect spot. Call him. Make sure those particular days are clear for the family. If it's during the week and you have kids, secretly arrange to have them stay with relatives or friends— as long as you're both comfortable leaving your kids with a sitter.

Give her as much notice as you think is necessary. Some highly structured women need more advance notice. Others can split on a dime. Then tell her what to pack and go. Have a great time and know that you've done an awesome job.

WHIP OUT YOUR CALENDAR

Plan ahead. Select a concert, a moonlight hike, a recipe you'll prepare for dinner, a day off for her at a day spa, or any number of other activities. Now open your calendar and map out one activity per month for the next six months.

Can you imagine how astounded she'll be when she realizes how much thought and time you've put into caring about her? All you're actually doing is your job—running the sex and romance departments. The truth is, all of this planning probably won't take you more than an hour or two. But it's more than you've done lately, right? And the impact will be enormous.

FIND CREATIVE NEW WAYS TO
SHOW HER YOU LOVE HER

Flowers are great. But if you bring them home every Friday, perhaps "the bloom is off that rose." In other words, it's time to mix things up, surprise her, surprise yourself. If you can't think of anything, ask a friend. Other men are great resources. They may be stuck too, but their old tricks may be new for you—and just what the doctor ordered. So, get off the couch, make the plans and follow through. Her newfound anticipation for your next innovative move puts you in the driver's seat, and gives her the chance to buckle up and enjoy.

LEARN THE SLOW BURN

If sex has become too fast, and too predictable, slow it down. Women tend to warm up slower than men. They often want you to take your time. Caress her skin. Cuddle. Touch and rub her in new places. Cover the sheets with rose pedals and lay her across your big brass bed. Get some body butter and work her into a lather until the slow burn becomes a full-on wild fire.

NEVER SAY NO! WHEN YOUR WIFE GIVES YOU THE SIGNAL, BE SURE TO HAVE PASSIONATE SEX—EVEN IF YOU'RE NOT IN THE MOOD

That mood is what will kill your relationship. Time, once again, to Silence the Little Boy—Tool #1. Hey, it's your job. What, you'd prefer she get it someplace else? Take care of your wife when she lets you know she's ready. Don't be selfish. Don't withhold. Go ahead and break through that immature barrier that's keeping you from intimacy. Once you push through, so to speak, the intimacy will return and you and your woman can get back on track.

IF YOU DON'T ALREADY, LEARN TO LOVE GOING DOWN ON YOUR WIFE

If you already know this one, up your frequency. For the uninitiated, you guys have to insist on it even if she initially pushes your head away because she "doesn't want to finish that way," or some other reason. You see, many women are uncomfortable about letting go and enjoying your selfless efforts, and some think it smells bad down there and are embarrassed or otherwise uncomfortable. Grab her out of the shower if that's what she's worried about, but get started. Tell her you love her and everything about her.

Once she experiences the full force of your endeavor, she will never push your head away again. And if you like her shaved, grab the shaving cream. Also, if you're not sure how long to stay "down undah," try writing the alphabet with your tongue, mate. That oughta get you an "A" in her Majesty's English.

READ MORE ABOUT IT

There are so many books about sex available today. Pick one up. You're bound to learn a thing or two. Then try it!

DON'T SETTLE

If sex isn't what you want it to be in your marriage, maybe you've come to the conclusion that there's really nothing you can do about it. Not true. Reread this book until you can reacquaint yourself with the vision of what you've always wanted your relationship—and the sex in your relationship—to be.

This may be the most difficult challenge you face because you're dealing with such an intimate aspect of your relationship. Ask for help from the men. Have a discussion with her about it—about how you feel and what you want—without making her wrong.

You may find the obstacles that have kept you from each other—from having the sex life you both want—were simply your own fears of rejection, and the lies and excuses you concocted to justify your lack of action. Don't settle.

CLOSE ALL BACK DOORS

If you intend to recommit to running the sex and romance in your relationship, you have to be willing to close your back doors—all of them.

As mentioned earlier, a back door is anything that diverts the energy that would have been directed toward your woman: online porn, full-release massage, hookers, and excessive masturbation, old girlfriends, and office flirtations, to name just a few. These activities are fulfilling a need, a need better fulfilled through an intimate relationship with the woman you love.

If you have trouble cutting back or eliminating one or more of these diversions, ask for help. Believe me, you are not alone.

IN A N.U.T.SHELL

LET'S RECAP RUN THE
SEX AND ROMANCE DEPARTMENTS:

- When she feels the love, she'll give you the sign. When she gives you the sign, it's all up to you.

- Close all back doors to endeavors that drain your sexual energy and distract you from your job at home. Don't expect the tide to turn until you make a real commitment and install a deadbolt on that back door.

- Cooperate with her and you'll find that running the sex and romance departments will get a whole lot easier.

- Intimacy comes from you taking the time to let her know what she means to you. And that takes a little romance.

- Cherish and protect her.

- To keep the marriage strong and the sex great, the romance must continue, forever. And that's your job.

- Fear of rejection belongs to the little boy. Don't allow that moody little boy to run your sex life. He'll screw it up!

- Be the man your wife would like to have an affair with.

- Ask other men for help, advice and suggestions.

- Be creative. Plan ahead. Don't settle.
- Keep moving forward by using the BetterMen Actions.

THE 8 BETTERMEN TOOLS

Nº. 1
SILENCE THE LITTLE BOY

Nº. 2
EXPRESS BUT DON'T DEFEND
YOUR FEELINGS

Nº. 3
COOPERATE WITHOUT
COMPROMISING YOUR N.U.T.s

Nº. 4
RUN THE SEX AND
ROMANCE DEPARTMENTS

► Nº. 5
BE THE ROCK ◄

Nº. 6
DON'T ARGUE

Nº. 7
LISTEN

Nº. 8
DEVELOP TRUSTING
RELATIONSHIPS WITH MEN

TOOL Nº.5

BE THE ROCK

One of the most important things your wife needs from you is to know that, no matter how she feels—no matter how angry, scared, sad, uncomfortable or frustrated she is, no matter how she acts or what words come out of her mouth—you will still be there when she's done.

She wants to be able to be who she is and know she doesn't have to be responsible—in those challenging times—for the way her behavior may affect you. If she has that freedom, and you don't run away, get defensive, try to fix her or her problem, or make it about you and argue, you will be much more the man she needs. You'll also probably get laid more frequently, and you'll be much happier in your marriage.

TIP!

Being the rock means expecting that she may not be at her best around the time of her period, and not letting her behavior cause you to get into an argument or force you to avoid her. She already feels bad enough, at least physically. Getting the message that she's "being a bitch" and somehow responsible for pushing you away is the last thing she needs. Do your job during this tough time for her and she'll show her appreciation.

That's being the rock.

Being the rock doesn't necessarily mean being stoic, expressionless or silent. It means being present and available for your wife without taking what she's saying personally—even if it's about you. It means doing the work you need to do so that you can be strong for her, especially when she really needs you to be. It means being a man when she's feeling or acting like a little girl.

WHEN TO BE THE ROCK

It's sometimes frustrating for men when their women are acting out. If a man receives an insult or some other hurtful comment from his wife, he finds himself in bit of a double bind. If he says nothing, he risks compromising his N.U.T.s and being a whipping boy. If he confronts her, he risks getting involved in an argument. What's a better man to do?

Under normal circumstances, it's perfectly acceptable to refer to Tool #2 and to Express Without Defending Your Feelings. But there are times when it's best not to express your feelings, to Be the Rock, and then allow her to bring it up to you later, when she's ready.

This dynamic is critical for a healthy marriage, and men can really use the support of other men—Tool #8—Develop Trusting Relationships with Men—to help sort out when it's a good time to speak up and when it's the right time to be the strong and silent type.

WARNING!

Being the rock doesn't mean stuffing it, being emotionally unavailable and acting like a robot. It means being able to listen to her without being distracted by the little boy screaming in your head. It means knowing that it's OK for her to feel and to say whatever she wants, knowing that her feelings have little or nothing to do with you.

When you're strong enough to not take her comments personally and to be a great listener, you'll be showing her how much you care and how safe she can feel when you're around. It can be tough at first, but you'll quickly see the rewards.

For instance, let's say she's having a rough day, she's worn out, and in her frustration she says something mean to you. Some women know right away when they're acting inappropriately and, depending on their upbringing, are already beating **themselves** up for "being a bitch."

If you reprimand her at that moment, it's like pouring salt on her wound, and she's likely to strike back. This is a tough spot for men. Essentially, she's not allowing you the satisfaction of telling her she's wrong—she's already taken care of that herself. It can be enormously frustrating. It's a real test.

YOU GOTTA KNOW YOUR WOMAN

Women, many of whom were raised by authoritarian fathers or in some sort of dysfunctional or abusive household, have a history of being made wrong. They've heard it so often they really don't need **you** or anyone else to tell them.

If you're married to one of these women, it's important to know how much she needs you to be the rock for her. It's your job not to react in that moment, to be the rock, to be patient. Chances are that after the tension subsides, she'll let you know—either by an apology, a look, or some other subtle cue—that she appreciates you not making a big deal of her behavior. Some proud women may be **extremely** subtle with their cues, so pay attention. And even if she

TOOLS IN USE

"My wife and I were not only on different pages, we were on different planets when it came to the issue of deciding where our son would/should attend college. Every discussion seemed to end in an argument.

My wife had (what I considered) an unreasonable (and wastefully expensive) expectation of how we should proceed. In her mind she envisioned a certain experience with ivy-draped buildings, quads, freshman year in the dorms. I felt it would be smarter to start out slower, maybe at a junior college. Then he could transfer and graduate to a more prestigious school than he would be accepted to now. To my wife, junior college sounded like a failure. And to me, that failure sounded like my failure. If we had more money, if I had been a better provider ... It pushed my buttons.

With the help of the men I began to see what was going on and how I could take a principled stand—and deal with this from a place of strength—once I worked through my insecurities about money, success and failure, and the other buttons I was allowing her to push. In other words, the men helped me through my stuff so I could "be the rock." It was only then that I could talk—rather than argue—with my wife and son, and work together to come up with a good solution."

— K.F.

doesn't show her appreciation—or you miss the signal—know that you did the right thing by being the rock.

This type of interaction will be a challenge for some men, especially those accustomed to argumentative relationships. But once you see it in action, you'll see how powerful being the rock can be and how much more secure she will feel being with you, especially when she's not at her best. Being the rock also gives you an opportunity to use some of the other Tools, like Silence the Little Boy, Listen and Don't Argue.

TIP!

> For all of us, men and women, we bring our childhood traumas, wounds and other issues with us into our relationships. Being the rock and not acting like her father—or some other abusive adult from her past—is like giving her a gift.

BEING THE ROCK WILL BE A TEST

Being the rock is also about holding on to your N.U.T.s. As we've discussed earlier, the challenges you'll face when establishing your N.U.T.s within an existing relationship will depend largely on your wife. If she's been waiting for

TIP!

Have you conditioned her to expect that if she pushes, pleads, complains, whines, screams, manipulates, tempts you with sex, or withholds sex long enough, you'll compromise your N.U.T.s and she'll get what she wants?

It's time to send a new message and to earn her respect. It's time to retrain her by being the rock and being consistent. It's hard to say how long it will take, or if she'll ultimately learn to trust and respect you. But being the rock, and holding on to your N.U.T.s, will help you to be the best man, husband and father you can be.

you to become that man she knows is inside, you'll receive less resistance than from the woman who is full of resentment, and who is not trusting of your efforts to change.

Remembering to be the rock will allow you to not react to the tests you will undoubtedly receive from her when you begin to make changes in your behavior. These tests are to be expected and are her way of checking to see how committed you are to holding on to your N.U.T.s.

She'll be checking to see, in any number of creative and infuriating ways, if this better man is here to stay—or just a passing fancy.

What might these tests look like? She may ask you to take care of a household chore you used to complain about and

WARNING!

Being the rock does NOT mean tolerating physical abuse. If that's what's going on, ask for help. You can call the police, find resources on the web, or ask men you trust for guidance. Domestic violence is intolerable no matter who the aggressor is. Be the best man you can be, stop being the victim or the perpetrator, and get help.

never do. She may surprise you with an unexpected "unloading" to see if you're really the consistent listener she needs. She may start what in the past would have been an argument to see if you still have that insatiable need to be right. She may do a lot of things—intentionally or unconsciously. If you apply the Tools, you'll "pass the tests," these challenges that will show her she can truly count on her man.

Now, passing the tests won't always mean she's happy with you. It's important for you to pass these tests as the man you want to be. Passing these tests means applying the Tools and never compromising your N.U.T.s. And as we've discussed, having terms won't always make her happy, at least not in the moment.

Remember, she'll feel more secure in your relationship when she comes to trust that you will be the best man you can be, and that you will be that man consistently. So, expect the tests and pass them as the man you want to be.

TOOLS IN USE

"I actually came for mentoring to figure out how to get out of my marriage. We had been married for ten years. We have one child together and two from our previous marriages. Although I wanted things to work out, it had been so unbearable for so long, I was ready to quit.

All I had were complaints about my wife. In my sessions, it was all about blaming her, until I finally understood what it meant to be the rock and decided to try it out at home.

I have to go to social events for work quite frequently. Because of our history, my wife tends to get suspicious or jealous. Well, on this particular occasion, I had to go and she didn't want to come with me. I asked her to, but instead she claimed to be sick and wanted me to stay with her. I committed to going and I really felt like she was trying to manipulate me. My problem is that when she is unhappy— and I was certain a tirade was about to be unleashed—I freak out and want to argue with her, convince her, or whatever it will take to make it stop.

This time I didn't get upset. I just told her I was sorry she felt bad and that I'd see her when I got back. I had a good time at this event and was proud of the way I had handled things. My concern was that I would get an ear-full when I got home. But when I got home, she was asleep. In the morning, it was like nothing had happened. I was confused, until I realized that I had passed the test. I had been the rock and, as a result, there was not a problem. Now I just have to keep being the rock."

— N.B.

TIP!

If you give her the power to make you miserable, she'll resent you for it. Don't give away your power!

A WORD ABOUT VERBAL ABUSE

Some men complain about their wives being verbally abusive. Certainly, if that's the case, you need to find a way to walk away from the situation until she's had a chance to calm down. On the other hand, you may have some work to do before you can accurately assess whether it's truly verbal abuse.

In my work with men and their wives, I've witnessed many interactions that appeared completely benign to me, only to hear the men characterize their women as verbally abusive. These moments gave the men an opportunity to see that what they were experiencing may have had less to do with their present relationships, and more to do with their past wounds. If you're experiencing this sort of dynamic in your relationship, take it to your men's group, a mentor or counselor. Find out whether it's actually verbal abuse, or some unresolved issue from your past.

Here are some BetterMen Actions to help you Be the Rock. Some of these suggestions will help prepare you to Be the Rock, while others are suggestions for when you are **in the line of fire**. Like the other Tools, take it slow and don't quit.

TIP!

When it comes to caring for her, being the rock requires that you improve your skills with Tools #1—Silence the Little Boy, #6—Don't Argue, and #7—Listen. When you do, it's much easier to be the rock because you've removed **you** from the equation. When you're no longer contributing to the problem, you're now part of the solution, and can be there for her completely.

BETTERMEN ACTIONS

JUST SAY NO TO FIGHT OR FLIGHT

Although in the heat of the moment it may feel as if your only options are fight or flight—arguing or running—neither one helps you to be the best man you can be. Instead, choose neither and see how it feels to simply be with her.

What comes up for you in those moments will be great material for you to share with the men or your counselor. Taking a look at these feelings of yours will give you insight into your issues, and help you to more effortlessly Be The Rock for her in the future.

FIND A PHONE BOOTH

The bullets are flying, figuratively. What she's saying is making you feel angry, frustrated, hurt or shamed. What to do? Do what Clark Kent would do: Shed those mild-mannered reporter clothes and reveal that colorful Superman outfit that lies beneath.

Bullets bounce right off of Superman. He doesn't have to fight back. It doesn't matter that Lois is ragging on him. He's so powerful Lois stops after a while and remembers how in love she is with her strong, indestructible—OK, except for the kryptonite—hero.

Life may not always feel like a comic book, but try being more powerful than a locomotive. She'll respond, perhaps not faster than a speeding bullet. But give her time. She needs to come to trust that you are a super-hero she can count on.

SEE THE HURT LITTLE GIRL IN YOUR WIFE

Just as you have the little boy to silence, she has her little girl. When she's having a hard time—even if she's taking it out on you, or it feels as if she is—try to see the hurt little girl behind her venom, her insults, her volume, her words or her tone. It will be easier for you to be the rock when you can see that needy little girl in your wife.

It's the same way you would want to respond to your little daughter or son if they were hurting and said or did something inappropriate or hurtful to get attention. Seeing that hurt little girl will help you to remove yourself from the equation and allow you to be there for her, to be the rock. And remember, don't tell her to silence her little girl. That's not your job and it won't help a bit. Just silently know it's what's happening for her.

IMAGINE BIG ROCK IN MALIBU

Just a few hundred feet off the coast in Malibu, California stands a large rock, the top of which rests above the surf. It has seen low tides and high tides. It has been hammered by storms, run into by water enthusiasts of all kinds, and crapped on by countless birds. That rock is still there and relatively no worse for wear. It has essentially been unaffected by its surroundings.

Spend a few minutes—preferably in a quiet spot—and think about that rock, or one you know of near your own home. Think about how the waves keep crashing into it and washing over it. Now, let the waves wash over you. Be that rock. Be that man.

HOW WOULD WILLIAM WALLACE RESPOND?

Watch *Braveheart*. Do you think William Wallace would get all bent out of shape when listening to your wife, hearing her needs, her complaints or the details of her tiring day? Of course not. But that's not to make you wrong. Maybe it can offer an example of the strong man, that rock, you can be.

William Wallace was able to weather attacks, fear, bloodshed and intense emotional and physical pain without ever forgetting who he was and what he stood for. He certainly had a firm grasp of his N.U.T.s. Be William Wallace for a day.

FAKE IT 'TIL YOU MAKE IT

This is a tried-and-true approach for any important life change. You may find yourself on uncertain ground as you try to implement these Tools into your life and into your relationships. If the vision of the man you want to be is to be that rock—that confident, strong and centered man—then act like him, even if it feels unnatural, unfamiliar or even wrong.

Paying attention will teach you about what works and what doesn't. With that insight, it will be easier and more natural for you to be the rock the next time. Eventually, you'll find that you're no longer faking it; you are that rock.

CONCERN YOURSELF WITH WHAT SHE NEEDS

Instead of paying attention to what you're feeling for a moment, pay attention to what she's saying, how she looks, what she's asking for or how upset, sad, anxious or angry she is. Try not to do anything except be a strong man who knows that it's OK for her to be just as she is and that you don't need anything from her at that moment. Just listen, care about her and be available to hold her when it's all over.

YOU DON'T ALWAYS NEED AN ANSWER RIGHT NOW

Being the rock means you can be OK with a situation, and be a source of strength and comfort, even when you don't have an immediate solution. We don't always have the information necessary to fix a particular problem or to relieve someone's pain or anxiety.

Being the rock means learning to be comfortable with uncertainty and having the faith to know the solution will come as long as you stay out of the problem. Providing that strength will make her feel more at ease, even if you have nothing to say or to offer at that moment.

Just be the rock and trust yourself. The solutions will come. In the meantime, you're being the strong, unflappable man she needs.

DON'T CAVE IN TO THREATS

More than one man out there has been repeatedly threatened with divorce—or tested by her with some other equally insidious threat—while bringing his newly developed N.U.T.s to his relationship.

It's particularly difficult to stand by your commitments—your non-negotiables—when she's threatening divorce, or worse, dragging your children into the battle. The best thing you can do for yourself—and to be a positive example for your kids—is to be the rock and not cave in. As long as you're clear about your intentions and your actions, being the rock—though potentially very painful—is your best option.

If you've been in a contentious marriage and she's hurt, resentful or has felt betrayed, she may test you to the breaking point. It's up to you not to break. She needs to see that you're committed to being this new man, this rock in the relationship. If this is your experience, go to Tool #8—Develop Trusting Relationships with Men—ASAP and get the support you need.

IF YOU'RE SILENT, MAKE SURE IT'S NOT PUNITIVE

There will be times when being the rock means saying nothing. Sometimes an important message can be delivered without words. There will be times when you're not sure what to say but your feelings are clear. In these moments, you must be sure that your silence isn't a form of punishment. Be certain you've silenced the little boy and you're not pouting or giving her "the silent treatment" to hurt her.

But once the message has been sent, it's important for you to let it go. At the next opportunity, engage in conversation and carry on with your life. She'll begin to see that this new man of hers means what he says and is capable of letting it go, not carrying a list, not holding a grudge and not arguing. Now that's a rock!

IN A N.U.T.SHELL

LET'S RECAP BE THE ROCK:

- She needs to know you'll always be there for her, no matter how she behaves.

- Don't run away, argue, get defensive, try to fix her or her problem, or make it about you.

- Being the rock doesn't necessarily mean being stoic, expressionless or silent. It means being present and available.

- Be the man when she's feeling or acting like a little girl.

- Being the rock, and by not acting like her father — or some other abusive adult from her past — is like giving her a gift.

- Being the rock, and holding on to your N.U.T.s, will help you to be the best man, husband and father you can be.

- Being the rock does not mean tolerating abuse of any kind.

- Pass the inevitable tests and she'll learn to count on her man.

- If you give her the power to make you miserable, she'll resent you for it. Don't give away your power!

- Don't cave in to threats.

- If you're silent, make sure it's not punitive.

- You don't always need an answer right now. Learn to be comfortable with uncertainty, and have faith the solution will come as long as you stay out of the problem.

- Keep moving forward by using the BetterMen Actions.

THE 8 BETTERMEN TOOLS

Nº. 1
SILENCE THE LITTLE BOY

Nº. 2
EXPRESS BUT DON'T DEFEND
YOUR FEELINGS

Nº. 3
COOPERATE WITHOUT
COMPROMISING YOUR N.U.T.s

Nº. 4
RUN THE SEX AND
ROMANCE DEPARTMENTS

Nº. 5
BE THE ROCK

Nº. 6
DON'T ARGUE

Nº. 7
LISTEN

Nº. 8
DEVELOP TRUSTING
RELATIONSHIPS WITH MEN

TOOL Nº.6

DON'T ARGUE

That's right. Don't argue with her. It's that simple. Have you realized yet that when it comes to arguing with your woman, **when you lose, you lose, and when you "win," you lose?** There is nothing to be gained from arguing that will, in any way, benefit you individually or as a couple. But you continue to do it. It may even feel, sometimes, as if it's out of your control. It's not.

We argue for very specific reasons. When we take the time to examine what's actually going on, we learn a lot about ourselves as men, and we learn how to communicate with our wives—and everyone else—without arguing. Once you master this Tool, you'll feel far more powerful,

TIP!

When in doubt, keep your mouth shut!

It's good advice and something we teach all Better-Men to do. If you'll give yourself the opportunity to think things through, or allow her to have her say without you reacting in anger, you'll begin to see new possibilities

At the very least, you'll buy some time to seek out help before making a mess of your relationship, again. Ultimately, you'll realize that there are better options for you, and for her. Give it a try.

and you may even get more enjoyment from simply talking with her.

This is how intimacy builds; it's what she really wants. You probably do, too.

THAT SUCKING SOUND YOU HEAR

So what is it that takes away all of your power and somehow sucks you into arguing with her? Some men hear their mother's voice every time their wife . . . raises her voice, gets angry, is negative, needs to be right, gets close to a reprimand, makes "that face," has "that tone," or even looks at him sideways.

TIP!

This Tool can help you elsewhere—in fact, everywhere. Once you learn to stop arguing with your wife, you'll realize how pointless it is to argue with anyone. The more effective route is to hold on to your N.U.T.s and to be the man you want to be. Once there, you'll find little reason to argue.

For some, this dynamic has been going on for so long he can't get a phone call from her or even come home after work without feeling that old tension in his gut. (And you know what? She knows when you're comparing her to your mother, and she absolutely doesn't like it, doesn't like you for it and sometimes doesn't like herself for being that woman.)

For other men, it's their experiences in their father's house that are at the core of their pain and the source of their arguing with their wives. Because of the fear, abuse or constant tension in their homes when they were boys, they grew to be men who will go to great lengths to avoid conflict. In their minds, anything that resembles their past can only lead to more hurt.

The problem is, these men oftentimes marry women who are just the opposite. She's more comfortable with

TIP!

Reprogram your cell phone.

If you find yourself annoyed when your wife calls, this tip may help you to change your behavior and, ultimately, your perspective.

Instead of entering a name like "home," "wife," or your wife's name to accompany her phone number, enter the word "opportunity."

Now every time she calls, you'll see an "opportunity" to use the Tools and to be the best husband you can be.

chaos and conflict; he'd rather hide his head. She ups the ante, he runs and she chases. (Of course, the opposite is also quite common.)

Eventually, his anger, rage and resentment are too much for him to keep stuffed. He explodes. At the very least, there's an argument. Sometimes, it's worse. After years of this behavior, it doesn't take much to push each other's buttons.

FEELINGS ARE FEELINGS, SO WHY ARGUE?

We, men and women, will engage in arguments to convince the other to change how they feel so we don't feel bad anymore. For instance, if she expresses a feeling that makes you feel ashamed, your first reaction may be to change her mind so that she won't feel that way anymore and, as a result, you'll feel better.

The problem is, it doesn't work. Why? You're probably dealing with very old feelings and trying to fix the past by changing each other in the present. It's what many of us do, but it doesn't make any sense.

Let's say, for example, she'd prefer you didn't drink as much as you sometimes do at dinner. (And let's assume, for discussion's sake, you're certain your drinking is not excessive.) She may be asking you to change because your drinking reminds her of her experiences with an alcoholic parent.

WARNING!

Some couples enjoy heated debates about topics that interest them, like politics, popular culture, etc. If these are the types of "arguments" you're having, that's fine. If it works for you, do it. But be sure it's something you both still enjoy.

Sometimes, the novelty can wear off and someone's afraid to tell the truth. If you find that certain topics seem to push someone's buttons, leaving either of you feeling hurt or angry, pay attention and stay away from those topics in the future. Again, if it isn't good for both of you, stop doing it!

You may not react as a gentleman because your experiences—perhaps having had a dad who drank too much—has made you overly sensitive to any suggestion that you have a "drinking problem." It's easy to see where this discussion is headed and how the inevitable argument can have more to do with old feelings, than with any real and present problem.

TOOLS IN USE

"When I argued with my wife I used to get really pissed off. I felt like I had to say something, even if it was telling her to "f@*% off." This was simply out of frustration because I couldn't argue with the same proficiency as her. I need time to mull over how I feel and trust the person to whom I'm saying it, which doesn't happen when I'm arguing.

One of the first Tools Wayne introduced me to was "Don't Argue." In a very simple way, this Tool has helped me keep my mouth in check and not say something I will regret later. By using this Tool, I have found how damaging my words were when I used to argue and how powerful it is NOT to argue. I don't mean that I won't express myself, but when I want to say something, it will be on my terms. If my wife or anyone else doesn't like that, which at first my wife didn't, I'm OK with that. I can stay in the moment and keep listening. Arguing was destructive to me and to the relationships with the people I love. I have even begun to pass this Tool on to my boys."

— P.C.

TIP!

> If she's telling you how she feels or you're sharing how you feel with her, there's nothing to argue about. If you find yourself wanting to argue, you're not really listening and what you're doing is trying to convince her to feel differently so that you feel better. Knock it off!

You can't **win** when you're arguing about feelings. We feel how we feel. The only way to feel better, long-term, is to learn why **how she feels** affects you so much and why you've given her so much power over you. You'll learn a lot about this as you put these Tools to use. But you may want to do more work with men you trust or in counseling.

In the meantime, just knowing this dynamic is taking place in your relationship may help you to see the value of embracing this Tool. If you don't argue, you'll help create an atmosphere where both of you can share the good stuff **and** the tough stuff that comes with long-term relationships and the responsibilities of a family.

TODAY'S ARGUMENTS ARE LINKED TO YOUR PAST

Perhaps you recognize yourself somewhere within this brief description and can begin to appreciate that what

WARNING!

Your problem is not: "We don't communicate," despite what you may have read in a magazine or a book on relationships. You're communicating, all right. The problem is what you're communicating is anger and resentment.

Once you stop arguing, you give yourself and your wife a chance to communicate some other ideas, thoughts and feelings. It may be difficult for you to imagine things going a different way with your wife. But once you stop arguing, something different will happen. Have some faith and give it a try.

underlies your tendency to argue has more to do with your past than with your present. You may disagree. But if you think back over the arguments you've had, you'll probably find that, although there may have been good reasons to discuss the issues, the arguments that ensued had little to do with the content and had more to do with your emotions and unconscious reactions.

The key to mastering this Tool is for you to **get conscious**.

- When you become aware of what's going on inside of you, it will be easier for you to stop yourself from arguing.

- When you recognize your need to be right, you can stop yourself from arguing.

- When you feel the little boy wanting to get back at his mother, you can stop yourself from arguing.

- When you realize you're not actually under attack or in harm's way—as you may have been as a boy—you can stop yourself from arguing.

- When you hear that what she's telling you is simply how she feels, you can stop yourself from arguing.

- When you can see how childish you're being, you can stop yourself from arguing.

On page 159 you'll find a series of BetterMen Actions that will help you to integrate this important Tool—Don't Argue—into your relationships and guide you to a place where arguing with your wife—or anyone else—is no longer an option.

TOOLS IN USE

"I was driving with my wife and child and decided to stop and get coffee. My son loves the whipped cream at the coffee shop. When I pulled over to park, my wife angrily protested, saying that we just stopped an hour ago at a different place. I turned to her and calmly said, "We have no plans for today and do not have to be anywhere. It is my day off and I am going in with my son to get coffee. You can stay in the car, or you can come with us, but we are going." She stayed in the car. My two-year-old son and I went in, sat down and enjoyed ourselves. He calls the whipped cream "ice cream." I did not rush at all. When we returned to the car 20-30 minutes later, she apologized for rushing me and admitted she was wrong.

Interpretation: In the past I would have tried to convince her through negotiation to get coffee, which would have been unsuccessful and frustrating. She would have gotten defensive, I would have gotten angry and a simple thing would have turned into a two-hour emotional festival. I wouldn't have said what I wanted and she would be right to be angry with me. The real kicker was the apology. I did not see that coming, but I learned that to get what you want, you need to have the courage to ask for it and remember to NEVER argue."

—S.C.

BETTERMEN ACTIONS

FOR ONE WEEK, DON'T ARGUE

This is actually one of the easiest Tools to implement, even without understanding why you've been arguing. There can't be an argument if you don't participate, no matter what she says or does. When you stop arguing, you'll see a remarkable change. You don't even have to read any further to try this one. Go home and Don't Argue with her. See what happens. Pay attention to what your body is doing and where your thoughts are going.

When you realize you have the ability to pay attention to what's happening in the room, rather than going into anger and losing yourself in an argument, you'll have made a huge step toward finding better ways to communicate with your wife.

It's this simple: Don't argue!

IF I DON'T ARGUE,
WHAT AM I SUPPOSED TO DO OR SAY?

You can let her know that it feels like you're heading toward an argument and that's something you're not going to do anymore. If she allows herself to hear you, maybe the two of you will be able to talk. If not, you may have to tell her that you'll be glad to talk with her about it, later, when you're both calmer.

Sometimes you simply have to show her how you feel. If being as reasonable as you can isn't enough to avoid an argument, then just walk away. If she chases you, keep walking. Stay focused. If you've made a commitment to honor this Tool, then you have to be willing to see it though.

At first, she may not respond well; it may cause her to get even more upset. It'll be difficult, but let it go. It's important for you not to judge your performance by her behavior. Meaning, just because she gets upset with you, doesn't mean you've done something wrong. She's not your mother.

Eventually, if you're consistent in your commitment not to argue, it will be easier for you to stay with her until she's willing to talk with you about how she feels, what she's afraid of, what's on her mind.

ABANDON YOUR NEED TO BE RIGHT

When you argue with her, prove your point, and make it crystal clear—at least in your own mind—that you're right and she's wrong, what happens next? Do you feel better about yourself? Does she?

More likely, you're full of adrenalin and hostility, she's taken a blow to her self-esteem and you're on the couch for the night. Worse, the relationship takes a big hit and the cumulative effect can destroy your marriage. Give it up. Stop needing to be right.

A better route may be to Listen to her—Tool #7—and then let it go. Perhaps she does have something to add. If not, does it matter? Is it really worth another round of "beating each other up" emotionally just to be right?

REVIEW PAST ARGUMENTS
AND FIND THE PATTERNS

What led to the argument? How were you feeling about her at the time? What was your state of mind? Were you tired, hungry, drunk, still upset about something else? What were you actually arguing about? Can you see yourselves described somewhere in this Don't Argue chapter?

Take a few minutes and see if you can connect some dots. You can't fix the noise under your hood until you know where it's coming from, and the same holds true here. The more aware you are of what causes that horrible screeching noise between you and your wife, the easier it will be to not argue next time.

JANE, STOP THIS CRAZY THING!

Ever feel like George Jetson on that space-age treadmill? You get into the same old arguments and you're screaming for someone to stop it. But no matter how loud you scream, it just keeps on going.

The only way to stop the arguing is for you to stop arguing. This is all about quitting a bad habit and committing to be the best man you can be. If you can keep your mouth shut long enough, you'll become aware of something else, some other feelings or thoughts. You may realize that you're angry, hurt, disappointed, or even hungry! If you take a breath, you may learn that this present situation is reminding you of an incident from your past, maybe with a parent, lover or friend.

Whatever that is, take it to the men or to your counselor. That's what progress looks like in this difficult but rewarding journey of becoming a better man. Some days it'll feel like baby steps; some days the light bulbs will go on. But for now, your first step is to stop this crazy thing. Don't argue. You have that power.

ARE YOU DEFENDING YOUR N.U.T.s?

Pay attention to what's actually being discussed. Are you defending one of your N.U.T.s? Are you being asked to compromise something you're committed to? If you're not sure, stop arguing and spend more time developing your N.U.T.s with a man you trust.

It's important to remember that there is no need to defend your N.U.T.s. These are non-negotiables, so why are you negotiating and arguing about them? When you hold on to your N.U.T.s.—and you are clear about them and committed to them—there is no need to argue, no need to defend. That confidence you display by not arguing is powerful enough to move your conversation away from an argument and toward something more productive.

IF YOU FEEL AN ARGUMENT COMING ON, STOP AND CALL THE MEN

Once you Develop Trusting Relationships with Men—Tool #8—the best thing you can do is to let them help you to become the best man you can be. You may resist because you don't want to impose or to look weak and in need. We're all weak at times, and we're all in need of each other's support.

When you feel your blood pressure rising, the knot in your stomach tightening or some other telltale sign that an argument is imminent, excuse yourself for a minute and call a man you trust. You'll be amazed at how powerful his words—and energy—can be. And since he's not emotionally involved, he can give you wisdom from a much calmer place.

You'll be equally amazed at how your perspective can change radically after connecting with a man who knows you and the changes you want to make in your life and in your marriage. Asking for help really works.

LET HER KNOW HOW YOU FEEL AND STOP THERE

A lot of men get into arguments because they don't do such a hot job with Tool #2—Express but Don't Defend Your Feelings. In other words, they don't know when to shut up.

Once you let her know how you feel, you can stop talking. That's right, you can stop talking. Your other options would be to

1. leave the room,
2. start defending your feelings and arguing, or
3. listen to her.

Ah yes, Listen. This is where Tool #7 can come in handy. These eight BetterMen Tools are interrelated. If used together, they can help you to show up more like the man and husband you want to be. If ignored, or not applied generously, you'll continue to find yourself right where you've been—stuck in an argument.

DON'T ARGUE ABOUT HOW SHE FEELS

Men argue with their wives when they hear something that pushes a button, something they don't like, or that makes them feel like they're being attacked. But most of the time, she's just telling you how she feels.

Now, she may not be great at expressing her feelings without including words you find objectionable, for one reason or another. But arguing with her will not help you change her or help her to get what she needs from you.

What she needs is to be heard. What you need is to learn to recognize when she's telling you how she feels. If you can keep yourself from arguing—and allow yourself to Listen—Tool #7—to her— you may find yourselves in an entirely new and enjoyable place. It's called a conversation! But first, you've got to stop arguing with her about how she feels.

THINK OF ARGUING AS AN ADDICTION

Have you ever tried to stop smoking, overeating, drinking, gambling or using? It's not easy. Those who succeed usually accept the support of others, and take it one day at a time. They don't quit when it gets tough, and they learn to forgive themselves when they slip. Perhaps it would help you to look at your habit of arguing as an addiction. If you approach it with that sort of seriousness and resolve, you'll be able to make this important change in your life.

Whether it's cold turkey or making gradual changes toward your goal, use the approach that best suits you, one day at a time.

IN A N.U.T.SHELL

LET'S RECAP DON'T ARGUE:

- When you lose, you lose, and when you "win," you lose.

- When in doubt, keep your mouth shut.

- You may hear your mother's voice every time she raises her voice, gets angry, is negative, needs to be right, gets close to a reprimand, makes "that face," has "that tone," or even looks at you sideways. Remember, she's not your mother.

- When you hold onto your N.U.T.s, you'll find little reason to argue with anyone.

- Silence the little boy by being aware of the childhood buttons being pushed.

- Expressing without defending your feelings reduces the tendency to argue.

- It's pointless to argue about feelings. Yours aren't "right" any more than anyone else's.

- Abandon your need to be right or to get even.

- If you find yourself wanting to argue, you're really not listening.

- When you feel an argument coming on, stop and call the men.
- If you don't argue, there's no argument. That increases the potential for greater intimacy.
- Keep moving forward by using the BetterMen Actions.

THE 8 BETTERMEN TOOLS

Nº. 1

SILENCE THE LITTLE BOY

Nº. 2

EXPRESS BUT DON'T DEFEND YOUR FEELINGS

Nº. 3

COOPERATE WITHOUT COMPROMISING YOUR N.U.T.s

Nº. 4

RUN THE SEX AND ROMANCE DEPARTMENTS

Nº. 5

BE THE ROCK

Nº. 6

DON'T ARGUE

Nº. 7

LISTEN

Nº. 8

DEVELOP TRUSTING RELATIONSHIPS WITH MEN

TOOL Nº. 7

LISTEN

You will need to become a good listener. There's no way around it. Listening is something you must learn to do better if you want to have successful long-term relationships. Your wife needs to have someone who will listen to her, care about her, offer her a shoulder to cry on, be there to complain to and laugh with, and to support her. You're it!

Or at least you should be. If you're not, you won't get the rewards, like intimacy, someone who loves and trusts you, a partner to have fun times with, and, uh . . . oh yeah, sex.

But you're thinking: "But I can't stand hearing her go on and on;" "She drives me crazy every time I come home and she dumps on me;" "I keep hearing the same stuff over

TIP!

Listening and multitasking are mutually exclusive activities. As the saying goes, "If a job is worth doing, it's worth doing well." This job, being a good listener, is worth doing well. So, walk away from the computer, turn off the TV, put down the newspaper and give her—and everyone else you care about—your undivided attention.

and over again;" or "I'm tired of hearing what a loser I am or how I keep doing everything wrong."

You're not alone. Long-term relationships present many challenges, and learning to be a better listener is one shared by most men. To make a change, it'll be helpful for

WARNING!

If she is being verbally abusive, tell her you will not discuss anything with her when she is being that way. Give her time to chill and tell her you'll be happy to talk with her about it later.

If she's being physically abusive, leave the house and—I'm serious about this—call the police. Domestic violence leads to more domestic violence. It's no more acceptable for her to abuse you than it is for you to abuse her.

TOOLS IN USE

"Early one evening after work, I came home to find her clearly disturbed about something—more likely, some things. I was clued-in by the usual passive-aggressive comments and subtle hints, like no eye contact and a heightened sense of urgency about doing simple tasks, like wiping the kitchen counter.

Upon trying to engage in conversation, I received an indirect invitation to a dispute, as she began to unload things I had done as recently as that a.m., to as historic as very early in our relationship—yep, she pulled out "the list." Typically, I'd be willing to take her up on the invitation by explaining, issuing counterpoints and ultimately providing potential resolutions. My approach, while serving me in my "business world," wasn't creating my desired outcome at home. Not by a long shot!

On this particular night, I reached into my tool belt— my wallet, where I keep a laminated card containing the "Tools"—assessed my available Tools, and implemented a very simple concept: I just listened! After she coughed up a bit more and still even MORE, I still just listened. When she finished sharing, expressing, and unloading, there was a pause. I walked over, embraced her, and let her know I had heard everything she had said—even reiterating some of her points that seemed to have the most heat.

I soon realized she hadn't even asked for me to respond— all she wanted was to be heard! I immediately abandoned my selfish need to respond in that moment. It was all about her. And for the first time, I was OK with that. After the hug, we went on to have a pleasant evening. In the past, it would have been a very different and chilly remainder of the evening.

The better news is that it wasn't a one-time aberration. Since then, listening has become a regular practice of mine. Yeah, my new Tool—Listening—has helped me build a bridge across what had seemed to be a huge gap in our relationship. Now we walk across that bridge together, and even enjoy the view."

— D.A.

---

you to understand what's keeping you from being the listener she needs.

The work you do will not only serve her, it'll help you to eliminate a tremendous source of frustration, anxiety and pain from your life. This work is vitally important for you, and it'll pay dividends for the life of your relationship—guaranteed.

LISTENING MEANS BEING PRESENT

Something happens for you in that nanosecond between the time she starts talking and the moment you stop listening. It happens so quickly—and it's been going on for so long, perhaps even before she came on the scene—that you don't even know when that moment has come and gone.

It's in that space, that instant in time—which normally goes unnoticed—where you'll find your answers. This is

WARNING!

Don't expect being a good listener today will earn you a get-out-of-listening card tomorrow. This isn't a board game. Your job is to be a good listener every day. The more you practice, the easier it gets.

where you'll find out what keeps you from being a good listener. This is where you'll learn what unconscious reactions make you want to argue, shut down, run and hide, fix, divorce, strike back . . . you name it. It comes down to being present, being in the moment.

Focusing on and understanding what you do in those moments—those nanoseconds—will not only help you to become a better listener, it will also help you to not argue, silence the little boy, and be the rock. That's half your BetterMen Tools!

GETTING TO THE SOURCE

What you'll find in those moments is any number of old wounds. You may hear your mother scolding you, or the voices of women who have come before. You may hear conflict and feel the old feelings you had when you were a kid and the victim of your mom or dad's—or someone

TOOLS IN USE

"My marriage fell apart—after 25 years—when my wife told me she no longer loved me. I was devastated. Now, two years later and with the divorce final, I'm learning about my role in a relationship that became unsatisfying for us both. Sure, there were a number of events and factors that ultimately contributed to the pain we both felt. But I can see now how my inability to listen to her was a key contributor.

There have been many times, in my present relationship, when my new woman has needed to talk, to be heard and to be cared for. She recently lost her father, she has career concerns, and then there's just the normal stuff she needs to purge. In listening to her—really listening and fighting the urge to fix and make things better—as I did for 25 years and not too successfully—I'm seeing how much easier it is for me and how much safer she feels being with me. She's even told me how great it is that I'm there for her and that I don't tell her what to do. I just listen.

It makes me laugh to think how easy it is for me now to be the listener she needs. It also makes me sad when I imagine what effect the use of this and the other Tools might have had on my marriage to my boys' mother."

— P.K.

else's—outbursts. You may feel like the little boy who never had his needs met, and so has little capacity to satisfy the needs of others.

TIP!

Assume for the moment that it's not about you. Without defending yourself or attacking her, just listen. You may find that although she begins her complaints directed toward you, the source of her crummy day may actually be something or somebody else. Just listen and wait.

Once you become aware of exactly what you're hearing in those moments, your head will be less cluttered. You will better understand what's going on, and what's been going on for such a long, painful time.

Once you can see what's happening, all it takes to make a change—to be a better listener—is a commitment from you. It takes your commitment to silence the little boy and to be the man in your relationship. It takes your commitment to be the best man you can be, and the best husband.

Think of listening as a wonderful gift you give to your wife over and over. It doesn't cost a thing, but the ability to listen is always at or near the top of a woman's list of things she most wants in a man.

Here are some BetterMen Actions to help you Listen. These suggestions will help you zero-in on those nanoseconds and better understand what's keeping you from being a good listener. They'll also help prepare you to be the best listener you can be.

BETTERMEN ACTIONS

BE IN THE MOMENT

One way to not talk—and at least appear to be listening—is to try to figure out what's going on for you in that moment that's making it so difficult for you to listen. Even if you're not paying attention to her words, just be there and pay attention to how you're feeling in your body—what's tense, what's your blood pressure doing, are you wanting to flee the scene, etc. See it. Then do nothing about it.

This exercise will show you that you can remain with her when she's talking. OK, so it's not being the best listener you can be, yet. That will come in time. For now, take small steps toward that ultimate goal. It can happen faster than you think.

DON'T TRY TO FIX

Your wife needs to be able to talk to you, for as long as she needs, without your editorializing or trying to help fix her. It may feel counter-intuitive, but the best fix is to not fix at all, just listen.

If you can listen long enough, and wait it out, you'll see that just having you there to listen to her was all the fix she needed. If she asks you for help or for an opinion, it might be wise to tread lightly. If you can just remember that she's more qualified to help herself than you are to help her, you'll be in good shape. Keep being with her and keep listening. She'll come to her own conclusions. And when she does, you'll look like a genius.

SWITCH GEARS

The skill set that makes you successful at work is not the same one that will make you successful in your personal relationships. You've probably experienced that already. To be the best husband you can be—and prepare yourself to be a good listener—it'll help if you find a way to switch gears before you come home from work.

Before you come into the house, take a few minutes (maybe drive around the block a couple of times or take five minutes to meditate at a park) and clear your mind of the day and all thoughts about you. Now, think about your wife and family. They had a day, too.

Take a deep breath, go into the house, and be available for your family. Ask your wife how her day went and then say nothing, until she asks you a specific question. Make it all about her. You'll be pleasantly surprised by the results.

REPEAT AFTER ME:
"IT'S NOT ABOUT ME, IT'S NOT ABOUT ME."

If she's in a particularly foul mood—good reason or not—it may be very difficult for you to patiently "take it" without giving in to the urge to retaliate with your own hurtful words. Don't. Here's a better suggestion. Just keep saying to yourself, "It's not about me, it's not about me, it's not about me." Try not to move your lips when you do it.

You may not actually be listening to what she's saying at that moment, but at least you're not talking, and you're keeping yourself from falling into old patterns. As a result, you'll have kept yourself from changing the course of her unloading, and you'll have managed to not contribute to what might have become an argument. Do this successfully for a while and you'll find yourself much more patient and capable of being that listener she needs.

DON'T ENGAGE

Listening helps to keep you from engaging. Engaging happens when you allow yourself to get sucked into her temporary mood. And it happens when you are drawn into her need—or your own—for conflict and chaos. If you participate with her rather than listen to her, you're adding fuel to a fire—and heading for an argument—that might otherwise have extinguished itself in a matter of minutes.

Next time you find yourself in the middle of what has traditionally been a firefight, remember not to engage and just listen. There's tremendous power in this technique. Best of all, you're doing your job and taking care of the woman you love.

DON'T NEED HER TO BE A GOOD LISTENER FOR YOU

You need to take your issues to men you trust or to your counselor, and just concentrate on being a better listener for her. When she begins to trust that you're really there and you really care, she'll be more attentive to you. But the key is for you not to need it so much.

Yes, you want to turn things around and have a better relationship with your wife. In time, that can happen. But right now, you have work to do. Being needy won't help you accomplish your goals. And think about it, do you want to be a man who is needy, or a man who knows what he wants and asks for the support of the men to help him get it?

WHERE SHE BEGINS MAY NOT BE WHERE SHE ENDS

If she's had a rough day and she's telling you what a jerk you were earlier in the day, if you wait and listen you may also discover more about her day: The kids drove her crazy, her mother laid some guilt on her, and her best friend disappointed her.

If you jump in to defend yourself, you're preventing her from telling you the whole story, depriving her of her need to unload. But when you listen, you end up being just what she needs.

LET HER KNOW YOU'RE PAYING ATTENTION

Once it becomes easier for you to be with her and to listen to her, let her know that you're actually paying attention.

One way to do that is to say something. It can be a "yeah" or an "uh huh." Even better are phrases that show real reactions, like "She/he really said that?" or "Wow, that's surprising" or "Sounds like it all worked out."

Another way to be a more active participant is to ask questions that encourage her to tell you more or to clarify something she said, like "What happened next?" or "How did that work out?"

Be careful how you apply this Action. What you say has to be authentic. Otherwise, it'll just sound like you read a self-help book and are blindly trying out a new technique. Let it come from the heart.

IN A N.U.T.SHELL

LET'S RECAP LISTEN:

- Listening is something you must learn to do better if you want to have successful long-term relationships.

- Listening and multitasking are mutually exclusive activities.

- Being a good listener today will not earn you a get-out-of-listening card tomorrow.

- Confusing your wife with your mother — or others from your past — prevents you from listening.

- Focusing on and understanding what you do in those moments — those nanoseconds — will not only help you to become a better listener, it will also help you to not argue, silence the little boy and be the rock.

- Even when it sounds like it's about you, it's not about you. Just listen.

- Switch gears before coming home. Take time to let go of your day, and make yourself available for your family.

- Don't try to fix her.

- When you talk, it's harder to listen.
- Think of listening as a wonderful gift you give to your wife over and over.
- Keep moving forward by using the BetterMen Actions.

THE 8 BETTERMEN TOOLS

Nº. 1
SILENCE THE LITTLE BOY

Nº. 2
EXPRESS BUT DON'T DEFEND
YOUR FEELINGS

Nº. 3
COOPERATE WITHOUT
COMPROMISING YOUR N.U.T.s

Nº. 4
RUN THE SEX AND
ROMANCE DEPARTMENTS

Nº. 5
BE THE ROCK

Nº. 6
DON'T ARGUE

Nº. 7
LISTEN

Nº. 8
DEVELOP TRUSTING
RELATIONSHIPS WITH MEN

DEVELOP TRUSTING RELATIONSHIPS WITH MEN

Women are terrific! Good women know how to care for their men. They can be partners, lovers and nurturers. Women can support their men and challenge them to be better men. But men these days are under the mistaken impression that women are supposed to satisfy their **every** need.

It's just not so. There are some things women can't do for us. And that's why we need other men who are also committed to this process of becoming better men.

If you want a reliable reflection of you as a man, uninfluenced by your or her wants, needs, desires and blind spots, you'll need to Develop Trusting Relationships with Men.

If your wife is your only source of support, you'll exhaust her and strain the relationship, whether you stay together or not.

You may think at the beginning of your relationship that you're all each other needs. You spend all of your time together, blowing off your friends. Eventually, you're wondering why you're so miserable and why you're resenting her. It's not her fault.

You need to connect with your men friends, or make new ones. Give yourself this gift, and give your wife a break. And while you're at it, support her when she wants to spend time with her friends.

Want to know how you're showing up? How others perceive you? If you're an insensitive moron or doing a great job? Only men who care about you, but have no vested interest in what you actually do with your life, can provide this mirror. These are men simply committed to supporting you to be the man you want to be.

We're not talking about men to just drink, smoke, watch sports or B.S. with, but men willing to go the distance with you; willing to challenge you when they know you're in pain but denying it; men willing to reveal their own pain and fear; men willing to hold you accountable to the commitments you've made to take care of yourself and your family; men willing to risk their relationships with you so you'll do the same for them. These are what we call **initiated** men.

INITIATED MEN

Initiated men are men who have learned to take off their masks—to reveal themselves honestly, without the protective covering most men put on to feel safe as they compete in the world. These are men who have made a commitment to learn about themselves as men, and to share what they have learned with other men. These are men who are in the process of doing their own "work," whether in counseling, men's weekends, in men's groups or through intensive introspection.

TIP!

Men's work, and the effort you make to become the man you want to be, is a journey. It may start with a men's weekend or men's group, but it won't end there.

It took you more than a few years to become the man you are today; it's going to take some time to change that man. So be patient. Celebrate your minor and major victories, give yourself a break when you screw up, and stay in relationships with men you can trust.

> An initiated man is a man who embraces his own masculinity, is comfortable with his place among the men, and is willing to mentor other men.

Initiated men understand the importance of holding men accountable to their commitments. These men are willing to risk pissing you off to help you be the man you want to be. They won't mother (comforting without challenging) you or simply try to make you "feel better" in the short term.

These men will listen, ask questions and challenge you to find your own answers. In other words, they'll **father** you and give you what you need to be a better man, husband and father. These men will be mirrors for you, showing you how they see you, and willingly participating with you to discover deeper truths within themselves. It always goes both ways.

Having men in your life to play with is necessary for every man. But having initiated men in your life will give you the support to become the best man you can be. By the way, having fun with these men—who are now your intimate friends and confidantes—will be the most fun you have ever had. There's nothing more thrilling than navigating river rapids or playing no-rules football with men

TOOLS IN USE

"I have a loving father, but one who never knew his own father while growing up. As I grew up (I'm 26), I never truly felt like a man. I didn't understand what that meant. I had no idea how to handle myself with women. In Robert Bly's (poet and men's work pioneer) words, I was truly a naive male. But that was before the men.

Since joining my circle of men over seven months ago—and experiencing the BetterMen Weekend, my life has gradually gained focus. How I view my interactions with people has evolved and matured. There has been so much change, in fact, that my life has seemed to explode in the past two months. I've had more first dates than ever before in my life. I've developed a stronger initiative at work. I've gone from being an introvert to seeing my own personality emerge. I've learned how to interact with other men and women in a way that works for me and for those around me. And I've learned to spend more time doing the things that make me happy.

All of this I've gained from joining a circle of men who meet weekly for 90 minutes. They've all been my elders, helping me to confront myself—my issues, my desires, my dreams and the plans for realizing them. Most importantly, they hold me accountable to my commitments and to the man I've told them I want to be. Their presence has allowed me to tune into the male spirit in a way I was rarely able to do in my adolescence. With their fathering, I've grown up. Thanks to this circle, I'm a man."

—— C.N.

WARNING!

Buddies vs. Initiated Men: Don't confuse buddies (guys you share activities with, such as work, or golf) with initiated men (with whom you can tell the truth and bare your soul). Having buddies does not constitute having initiated men in your life. There's a big difference. But once you experience and appreciate the difference, you may find you have the power to encourage your buddies to become initiated men.

whom you know—and know you—inside out. They've really "got your back."

If you're relying only on women for feedback, you're definitely not getting all of the information you need. Even if you are getting good feedback (and there are a lot of good women out there supporting their men) you may not be hearing it in a way that's helpful.

Let's say you're listening to a woman telling you how she feels about you, but all you're interested in is getting in her pants. Are you really going to hear her? And will you really tell her the truth about you? What if it's your wife giving you advice on how better to interact with your parents, but the last time you had this conversation it blew up into a huge fight? Are you going to be able to really hear her, or will your resentment get in the way?

But tell the men about it and they'll help you see it in perspective, without all that baggage surrounding it. You won't believe how helpful it is to be able to see yourself and your relationships for what they really are. You'll find yourself thanking the men for telling you the truth—good or bad. Why? Because now you'll know what to do to be the man, husband and father you want to be.

> Buddies will empathize where initiated men will call it as they see it and lend you the support you need to grow.

Initially, it will take time to understand your personal issues and how they affect your interactions with the other men. For example, you may find yourself holding back because that's what you do in your marriage to avoid a fight, or in life to "be liked." Once you realize that initiated men aren't concerned whether your words hurt their feelings, you're free to let it out and loosen up. Once you gain that insight, you'll have an opportunity to get the feedback you need and the support you can use to be the man you want to be.

TIP!

The last thing men want is to be seen as vulnerable, in need, or not having it all together. But when we're feeling that way, that's when we need each other most.

So, pick up the phone, get in your car or walk down the street. Tell your pal what's up and give him the gift of being there for his good friend. Sometimes just getting a little feedback is all you need to get back on track. And then maybe he'll realize that you'll be there for him when he's in need.

If you already have buddies, then you may have a jump on realizing stronger, more trusting relationships with them, although not all buddies have the courage to become initiated men. You may want to tread lightly and give your buddies some time to warm up to the notion of having a new and more intimate relationship with you.

If you don't currently have trusting relationships with men, you'll want to seek them out. You'll find some suggested ways to do that on the following pages.

TOOLS IN USE

"I was trapped in a loveless marriage of over 12 years. I cannot tell you how often the thought of divorce had entered my mind. I had unhappiness, but I lacked courage—the courage to divorce or the courage to find a way to improve my marriage. Then I received an email newsletter from the West Coast Men's Center.

The email announced an open house for men who wanted to make changes in their relationships and in their lives. Perhaps what I lacked in courage I made up for in desperation. So I went.

That night I sat in a circle with men whom I had never met and within minutes, I was crying. The floodgates had opened. I experienced something for the first time. It was the freedom that comes with opening up to men and getting unconditional support. I was embarrassed that evening because I felt I had monopolized the time and acted like a crybaby. I learned later what a tremendous impact I had on the other men.

That was two years ago. I know now that that first evening was the beginning of a whole new life for me, and an entirely new relationship for me and my wife. The men saved my life and my marriage, and helped me to be the father I had always wanted to be.

I cannot stress enough how important the feedback from the men has been for me. When I met the men, I was terribly unhappy and on the brink of divorce. That has all changed. Now I do everything I can to introduce what I have to my men friends. The power of being with the men cannot remain a secret. There is just too much need out there. And to think, for me this all started with an email."

— B.H.

What follows are BetterMen Actions for the Tool: Develop Trusting Relationships with Men. These are recommended ways to go about getting the support you need from other men to hold on to your N.U.T.s and to integrate your BetterMen Tools into your relationships.

BETTERMEN ACTIONS

FIND A MEN'S CENTER OR
MEN'S GROUP IN YOUR AREA

Participating in a men's group is a great way for you to throw your-self into relationships with other men. In no time, you'll learn a lot about yourself, realize you have more in common with other men than you ever thought, and begin establishing strong and trusting relationships with other men. You may even find a good friend while you're at it. And because the BetterMen Tools are not widely known, you may want to introduce them to your men's group to see what comes up, or use them as a guide to support each other.

You may have never realized it, but there are a lot of other men in your community struggling with the same issues that have caused you to get stuck in your own stuff. Most of these men struggle by themselves, but some of them have organized to help each other. You may find a men's center that offers a variety of groups, as well as other activities and services specifically designed for men.

In other areas, you may find men's groups facilitated by a coun-selor. There are "leaderless" groups that operate without a facilita-tor. And you may also find men's groups affiliated with churches and temples.

Find a place that feels good to you, a place with men who are willing to be vulnerable with each other in their efforts to become better men, and who don't want their relationships with other men to be sugar-coated. Search for a center or group where the philosophy encourages you—and even challenges you—to make the changes you want to make.

There are religiously affiliated groups that will expect you to be a man as defined by their "book," and that may not suit you. Other groups may not respect confidentiality, i.e., they'll share what's said in your group with their wives and girlfriends. So be picky. Find a group that makes sense for you. Use the Internet or ask others for referrals and don't quit until you find the right fit. If you can't find a men's group, start your own.

SIGN UP FOR A MEN'S WEEKEND

A men's weekend is probably the fastest way to immerse yourself in men's work and to connect with other initiated men in your area.

There are many men's organizations across the country offering men's weekends, retreats and other experiential opportunities. It's at retreats like these where men become initiated into the community of men. This is where you dig deep, truly learn about yourself and others, and begin the process of becoming the best man you can be. In addition to religious organizations, there are secular groups that support men to make important changes in their lives, like the work we do at our BetterMen Retreats.

FIND A MAN TO MENTOR YOU

If one-on-one counseling feels more like your speed, find an initiated man to do it with. Too often, men reach out to women to help them with their problems. But we don't need mommy any more. We need dad. The father energy we receive from our relationships with men— mentoring—is what will help us to become the men we want to be.

It may frighten some of you or feel very uncomfortable. Allow those feelings to drive you toward men rather than away. We need to seek those things we fear. It's a sign that there's something there for us to receive and to learn. Whether he's a mentor, therapist, counselor, or clergyman, find an initiated man you can trust and then allow that mentoring relationship to help you become the man you want to be.

Remember, just because he has a penis doesn't mean he's connected to his own masculinity. Many men who offer their services as therapists and counselors have not done their own men's work; they're not initiated men. Simply having a degree in psychology isn't enough. You want to find a man who has participated in his own men's weekends and men's groups; a man who understands and appreciates the differences between men and women and who can teach you some of the lessons you need to be successful and happy as a man.

To find that man, ask around. Search the web. Do some interviewing. See if what he says jibes with what you're learning from this book. Ask pointed questions. Most importantly, pay attention to your own body and emotional reactions when you're in his presence. Can you learn to trust this man? Are your first impressions positive? Does he appear to believe what he's saying or does he seem full of it? Does he have strong male energy, or does he seem too "soft" to be your mentor?

You may have a lot to learn about yourself as a man, but now's as good a time as any to start trusting your instincts. If you end that first session feeling a connection with that man, come back again. If the vibe is uncomfortable, or is just flat, keep looking. Trust your gut to help you find a strong and compassionate mentor. One place you can start your search is at www.Mentor4Men.com.

FIND THE MAN IN YOUR BUDDY

If you don't put effort into developing intimate relationships with men, no one will do it for you. Tell your buddy what's going on and how you really feel. Share your heartache, your problems, your pain and your wins. Let him know who you are and be there to listen to him. It may be hard for you. It may be hard for your buddy. But go ahead and take a risk!

Have coffee once a week. Go camping. Hit some golf balls together. Men have an innate desire to reach out and connect with other men, although our learned behavior might suggest otherwise. By taking a risk and revealing the man you want to be, you'll be giving your friend permission to do the same. Sometimes, that's all he'll need.

BURN YOUR LIST AND MOVE ON

You probably use lists to organize your life. But did you realize that you keep lists for other, less productive reasons? Lists are also what we create to keep track of our resentments toward others. They're what help us organize our petty and destructive thoughts. These lists help us to be right and to make the other guy, or gal, wrong. Lists keep us stuck. We don't need them; we don't want them.

So, take a few minutes, by yourself in a quiet place, and write down all of the reasons you don't like men, all of the times they betrayed your trust, all the hurtful experiences you had when you were a boy, and every other possible reason, excuse or explanation you've been carrying that has kept you from having men in your life. Take your time, maybe over the course of a few days or even weeks.

When that's done, take a match and burn the list as you say, "The man I want to be does not have room in his life for this list, so I'm burning it and moving on." This a cleansing ritual in which you burn away the old ways and make room for the man you want to be. This is the time to recognize and to let go, not to blame. Then pat yourself on the back and commit to one of the other BetterMen Actions suggested to help you Develop Trusting Relationships with Men.

And while you're at it, take some time to consider the "lists" you have on other people in your life, like your wife. It might be a good idea to burn those lists too.

CALL YOUR DAD

Is your dad, or the man who played that role for you, still around? When was the last time you called him? When was the last time you asked for his advice, even if you didn't think you really needed it? When was the last time you thanked him? Make a call.

This is your chance to honor him and to build upon an existing relationship with a man who loves you. This is a great foundation from which to start new relationships with other men. Go ahead and flex that muscle with a man you know and trust. You may know more about intimacy with men than you've given yourself credit for. Give him a call, and be vulnerable.

WHAT ABOUT THOSE OLD BUDDIES?

You know, the boys you used to play ding-dong-ditch with, the high school friends you used to cruise with on Friday nights, and the old college buddies who've probably all traded in those keggers for co-ed baby showers. As they say in business, it's easier to keep an existing client than to find a new one. Reconnect with old buddies and see if there's still a reason to have a relationship with them. You may be surprised.

HAVING TROUBLE THINKING OF WAYS TO MEET MEN?

Take an inventory of your personal interests. Maybe it's a sport, a hobby or a community concern. There are meetings, seminars, classes, rallies and many other forms of gatherings where you're sure to meet other men who at least have something in common with you.

The truth is, besides the issue or interest bringing you together, you probably also share a longing for deeper relationships with other men. But don't expect them to reveal that to you right away. Give it time. The important thing is to get off the couch and start making an effort to connect. Reveal a little of yourself and you'll give the other man permission to do the same—even if he doesn't do it right away.

SPREAD THE WORD

A terrific way to forge closer relationships with men is to open up and share with them what it is you're doing to become a better man.

You can break the ice by sending each of them a copy of *Hold On to Your N.U.T.s.* Sharing this book will give these men insight into what you're up to, give them an opportunity to reflect upon their own relationships and the men they want to be, and help you to develop trusting relationships with these good men.

IN A N.U.T.SHELL

LET'S RECAP DEVELOP TRUSTING RELATIONSHIPS WITH MEN:

- Women are terrific. But you NEED men in your life.
- If she's your only source of support, you'll exhaust her and strain the relationship.
- Only initiated men—men willing to go the distance with you—can be the mirror you need to see the kind of man you really are, and help you to make important changes in your life.
- Don't confuse buddies with initiated men.
- The men will teach you and help you to become the man you want to be.
- Surround yourself with men who will hold you accountable to your commitments.
- If you're relying only on women for feedback, you're definitely not getting all of the information you need to be the best man you can be. Choose fathering over mothering.

- Find a men's center, men's group or an initiated mentor.
- Reconnect with your men friends.
- Don't allow fear and resentment to keep you isolated.
- Call your dad. Be vulnerable.
- A men's retreat is the fastest way to immerse yourself in this work.
- Keep moving forward by using the BetterMen Actions.

AFTERWORD

A FEW FINAL THOUGHTS ON BECOMING A BETTER MAN

If you've read *Hold On to Your N.U.T.s* from start to finish, you may find yourself a bit overwhelmed with the amount of work required of you to be a better man in your relationships. On the other hand, you may have found just the Tool you need to get your relationship back on track.

If your head is swimming and you're not sure how to get started, relax. For most men, this information is completely new, and it'll take some time for it to sink in; it'll take some effort to develop your N.U.T.s. Give yourself some time and don't quit! Perhaps this final reminder will help you:

In any given situation or relationship, when confronted with a challenging decision, ask yourself this question: If I was the man I wanted to be right now, what would I do? Take the time to ask yourself this important question as often as you can. Then do it. In time, you will become that man.

Becoming a better man, husband and father is an honorable pursuit and one that is crucial for the health of our families, communities and society. It deserves your uncompromising commitment to your N.U.T.s, your unwavering use of the BetterMen Tools, your patience and your courage.

This book has detailed the connection between your N.U.T.s and becoming a better man, given you the BetterMen Tools you'll need to be that better man in your relationships, and explained the patience required to see you through this important process. The courage . . . is up to you.

Good luck becoming a better man. We need you!

But before you go, consider making a list of the men in your life. Would they benefit from the Tools in this book?

If so, go online and order a copy to be sent directly to them. It just might change their lives . . . and help you to develop more trusting relationships with men.

Now, go be the man you were meant to be!

ABOUT BETTERMEN

BETTERMEN.ORG

At BetterMen.org you will find the support you need to make important changes in your life and to become the man you want to be. BetterMen.org offers links to Mentor-4Men.com, the BetterMen Retreats, the West Coast Men's Center and a link to purchase additional copies of *Hold On to Your N.U.T.s.*

MENTOR4MEN.COM

Mentor4Men.com gives you the opportunity to tap into the BetterMen Tools from the privacy of your home or office.

Mentor4Men.com offers you the individual support you need to successfully integrate the material in this book into your life, to be the man you want to be at home, at work and in all areas of your life. You can do this work on the phone, in private, and with a guarantee of full confidentiality.

To read what men have to say about the Mentor4Men process, or to schedule your private mentoring session, visit www.BetterMen.org.

THE BETTERMEN RETREATS

Wayne M. Levine, M.A. created the BetterMen Retreats—with his team of initiated men—to give all men an opportunity to be initiated into manhood, and into the BetterMen community—a community of men committed to using the BetterMen Tools to become better men, fathers and husbands.

Everything that happens at the BetterMen Retreats teaches men something about themselves as men and something about their place in the community of men. The central message men receive is about the necessity of having men in their lives so that they get the support they need to make their changes to be the best men that they can be.

Everything men experience at the BetterMen Retreats, every exercise, ritual and game, is a tool that can be used over and over again as they strengthen their relationships with other men.

Although each man comes to the BetterMen Retreats with his specific life challenges in mind and some sort of expectation for addressing those needs, and although those issues will be addressed, the BetterMen Retreats primarily focus on developing the ability to be in relationship with each other. For without the men to hold each other accountable, to mentor each other and to care for one another, the likelihood of any individual man accomplishing his goals is greatly diminished.

At the conclusion of the BetterMen Retreats, rather than leaving in an altered state of seminar bliss, it is hoped that men leave invigorated but firmly planted in their masculinity. We want men to know more about themselves as men, to learn specific Tools they can use immediately to be the men they want to be at home, at work and in their communities, and to understand the process that will keep them connected to the men with whom they have shared this powerful initiation into manhood.

To register for the next BetterMen Retreat, visit www.BetterMen.org.

THE WEST COAST MEN'S CENTER

The West Coast Men's Center in Agoura Hills, CA provides mentoring services to support men and their families.

Men need to know there's nothing wrong in asking for help. We've been trying to do everything by ourselves for too long and it doesn't work. At the West Coast Men's Center, we've got a better way.

We mentor each other. We help each man to create a vision of the man he wants to be. We teach him how to use Tools that will help him to be that better man. And through our individual mentoring, BetterMen groups and BetterMen Retreats, we allow each man to experience the power of finding his place among the men.

Being the best man you can be takes time. After all, it took men quite a few years to arrive in the place they're in today. Through the support of initiated men, we grow up, we change, we improve, and we get closer and closer to being the man, father, husband, friend and mentor we've always wanted to be.

The BetterMen process isn't therapy. What most men need is not a diagnosis. What we need is trusting relationships with other men, to make commitments to be Better-Men, and to be held accountable to our commitments. This is what changes men's lives. This is what improves the lives of those we love.

For more information about the services offered
by BetterMen.org, or to purchase additional
copies of Hold On to Your N.U.T.s, visit:
www.BetterMen.org

Call or write:
West Coast Men's Center
5310 Derry Ave., Suite A
Agoura Hills, CA 91301
(818) 879-1600

For inquiries regarding special orders, volume discounts,
teacher or class discounts, or to arrange a speaking
engagement featuring Wayne M. Levine, M.A., email:
info@BetterMen.org

ABOUT THE AUTHOR

WAYNE M. LEVINE, M.A. is the director of the West Coast Men's Center in Agoura Hills, CA, where he coaches and mentors men, and facilitates men's groups. He also created the BetterMen Retreats for men, and for fathers and sons. In addition, Wayne is the founder of Mentor4Men.com, a life coaching and mentoring resource for men.

Wayne's interest in men's issues began in the early '90s with his participation in men's work activities. His experiences with men's groups, as a participant, leader and program developer, taught Wayne to "father" men and to support them in making difficult and important changes in their lives.

He earned his Master's in Clinical Psychology from Antioch University/Los Angeles. Wayne also received his BA in journalism and graduated Magna Cum Laude and Phi Beta Kappa from the University of Southern California.

Wayne's been married to his first and only wife, Ria, for over 20 years and is the proud daddy of Emma, Austin and the family's menagerie of animals. Wayne strives to be a better man, husband and father each day in Oak Park, CA.